BREAK-THROUGH

DAVID NURSE

BREAK-THROUGH

A Sure-Fire Guide to **Realizing Your Potential, Pushing Through Limitations, and Achieving Things You Didn't Know Were Possible**

WILEY

Published by John Wiley & Sons, Inc., Hoboken, New Jersey.

Published simultaneously in Canada.

For general information on our other products and services or for technical support, please contact our Customer Care Department within the United States at (800) 762-2974, outside the United States at (317) 572-3993 or fax (317) 572-4002.

Wiley publishes in a variety of print and electronic formats and by print-on-demand. Some material included with standard print versions of this book may not be included in e-books or in print-on-demand. If this book refers to media such as a CD or DVD that is not included in the version you purchased, you may download this material at http://booksupport.wiley.com. For more information about Wiley products, visit www.wiley.com.

Library of Congress Cataloging-in-Publication Data

Names: Nurse, David, author.
Title: Breakthrough : a sure-fire guide to realizing your potential, pushing through limitations, and achieving things you didn't know were possible / David Nurse.
Description: Hoboken, New Jersey : Wiley, [2022] | Includes index.
Identifiers: LCCN 2021039323 (print) | LCCN 2021039324 (ebook) | ISBN 9781119853930 (hardback) | ISBN 9781119853954 (adobe pdf) | ISBN 9781119853947 (epub)
Subjects: LCSH: Leadership. | Problem solving.
Classification: LCC HD57.7 .N866 2022 (print) | LCC HD57.7 (ebook) | DDC 658.4/09—dc23
LC record available at https://lccn.loc.gov/2021039323
LC ebook record available at https://lccn.loc.gov/2021039324

Cover image: Paul McCarthy
Cover design: Getty Images | Eyematrix
SKY10030305_101321

To my wife, Taylor, the biggest breakthrough of my life was marrying you. And every day keeps getting better and better!

To Jon Gordon, the brother, the mentor, the amazing light you are to the world. Thank you beyond words!

Contents

FOREWORD

by Jon Gordon

This past year I was named one of the top ten speakers in the world and had four books on the bestseller list at different times. Friends and colleagues reached out and commented on my breakthrough success. For many others, it looked like an overnight success. But if you know anything about success and breakthroughs, you know they don't happen overnight. They happen after years of hard work, dedication, and a commitment to living and sharing your passion and purpose.

Speaking of breakthroughs and purpose, I believe the greatest breakthrough of your life is finding your purpose. My purpose is to encourage and inspire as many people as possible, one person at a time, to create a more positive world. I say one person at a time because it starts within each one of us and for many it's not easy to be positive. I'm proof of this. Positivity doesn't come naturally to me.

My breakthrough actually began with an ultimatum from my wife, Kathryn: if I didn't change, she would leave me. It jump-started my work and my entire life, but not overnight. I didn't have a system to follow or a path planned out. I had a whole lot of trial and error. I had to construct my own system and process for breakthroughs. What I landed on, what worked best, was, in essence, the breakthrough formula David elaborates on in this book.

It took me awhile to accept that I need to work on my breakthrough every day. My breakthrough into positivity is as much a daily practice as brushing my teeth. I don't always look forward to it, but I know it is essential for my health, my marriage, and my career.

Early in my breakthrough, I wrote my first book, *The Energy Bus*, in a three-and-a-half-week fit of inspiration. It wasn't an instantaneous bestseller. I kept working on the breakthrough process every day and after five years, it finally became a bestseller. Now, fifteen years later, it still appears on the bestseller lists.

Since *The Energy Bus*, I've published a total of twenty-four books, and twelve have become bestsellers. It's a testament to the power of my breakthrough and the service I can provide to a world that needs positivity. It's an even greater testament to the people I work with. Without the ultimate team around me, I couldn't do anything that I do today—from my publishers at Wiley to my editors and advanced readers, and each and every person who reads my books. And, of course, to my beautiful wife, Kathryn, and my amazing family. The greatest breakthroughs don't just happen alone. They happen in cooperation with the team you have around you. If I didn't surround myself with great people who support me and are willing to challenge me, none of this would be possible.

One of the most rewarding parts of my life is being part of other people's breakthrough teams. I believe we are all called to be mentors and share what we have learned to help others grow. When I met David Nurse four years ago, I saw something rare in him. But truth be told, we didn't become fast friends. I needed to know he was on an actual mission for a bigger purpose. I kept my distance.

Despite my reservations, David would text me to check in, to see how I was doing, to just ask if there was any way he could serve me or help me with anything. He never asked anything for himself, just offered to give. After a while, I was too curious to keep my distance. Who was this guy? And why did he keep staying in touch?

I took David out for dinner, and I knew immediately what made David so different. Positivity. Optimism. They come naturally to David. They pour out of him, and it's infectious to be around. From epic three-hour tennis battles, road trips to NBA games to watch our friends coach, or just eating great food together and trying to solve the world's problems, I am proud to help David grow his mission. His natural positivity also helps refine and shape who I am. Iron sharpens iron.

David is a breakthrough waiting to happen. His gifts allow him to bring out the best in others. David is a great leader, a powerful author, and a person on a mission to show people how to experience their personal breakthroughs. Once you open yourself up to his system, you won't just experience a breakthrough. You will *be* the breakthrough.

Life is a series of breakthroughs, from breaking through in our marriages and finding true unconditional love with our spouse; breaking through in our faith and discovering a true personal relationship with God; and breaking through in our careers, harvesting the fruit of all our relentless labor. It can never be just given to us, and it sure doesn't happen overnight. Those of us who are committed to breaking through usually go through a lot of trial and error to reach a single point of clarity. David's mixture of drive and optimism helps him construct the universal formulas that help you experience regularly occurring breakthroughs. In reading this book you will see and understand exactly what I'm talking about.

The life you have always wanted to live is waiting for you to break through. Let this be your breakthrough moment.

FOREWORD

by Taylor Kalupa

I know every career relies on breakthroughs to flourish, but Hollywood actors are as dependent on them as comic book superheroes. You can be the most talented, most captivating, best-positioned person on the planet, but you just don't have a career until you catch the attention of an agent, a casting director, or a unicorn.

I caught my first Hollywood breakthrough opportunity starring in Dave Navarro's "Rexall." Though I was only ten, I joined a long list of stars who were introduced to the world in music videos—a club that includes household names like Matthew McConaughey, Eva Mendes, and Courtney Cox. I remember standing in line at Disney World shortly after it premiered on MTV; multiple teenagers and adults stopped me to tell me they recognized me. And kids at my elementary school excitedly ran up to me at recess to say they saw me on TV the night before.

But breakthroughs are bigger than just opportunities—getting a shot at the biggest stage on earth doesn't propel you into the skies if you don't nurture your talent, your team, and your purpose. Whether someone gave us our first chances to shine because of our extraordinary talent, our intensive training, our physical appearances, our last names and connections, or simply because we were standing in exactly the right spot at the perfect time, it was up to us to make the most of those breakthrough music video opportunities and turn them into lasting breakthrough roles.

Admittedly, I didn't. I wasn't that interested or invested. Even though I grew up with the bright lights of Hollywood in my backyard and had my first breakthrough opportunity in grade school, I didn't dream about seeing my name up on marquees. Actually, my most notable childhood dream was of my future husband. He wasn't anyone I knew; I didn't even have a super clear view of his face. But I would always remember his kind, bright golden-green eyes.

No, it took another twelve years before I was bitten by the acting bug. I'd already earned a business degree and was on the path to becoming a lawyer, so when I set my sights on securing my own Hollywood star, I needed to hustle and build my momentum back up from scratch. I needed to prepare my life for the next breakthrough opportunity; without a guarantee or a system (much less a well-constructed formula!), there were times when getting ready for the breakthrough was a real struggle.

November 2017 was rough. I was stuck in the revolving studio doors, auditioning for pilots I rarely heard back from. I'd taken over casting an entire project for a friend while she was on leave, so I was working endlessly long days. I was trying my best to produce a true story movie with zero experience and no real guidance or connections. And I was being treated for Lyme disease, which, thankfully, was caught early, but nevertheless struck me hard. Time and energy were at a premium.

I was memorizing another scene for an audition the next day when I got a text from a guy I'd known in college—sort of. Rich had been on Pepperdine's basketball team while I was on the dance team, so we'd really more known *of* each other. I had helped Rich in the past by answering questions for his younger brother about how to get into acting, but we'd never been great friends and we hadn't spoken in two years. I'll admit it—I groaned when I read, "Hey Taylor, I have a buddy who wants to get into acting. Would you be able to meet with him and give him some pointers?"

Not one part of me actually wanted to meet up with the type of oblivious stranger who asked friends of friends of acquaintances vague questions like "How do you get into act-ing?" I had less than no time and I was well into an energy deficit, and I couldn't imagine how to find more of either one to politely explain what it really takes and how rare it is to even get a role in a show.

But I'd committed to living in service mode, to giving when-ever I could. I spent day after day asking strangers to give me a shot, to help me improve, to stake their success on my efforts—and if I couldn't find the time and energy to serve this stranger who was asking the same of me, how could I keep asking it of others? I agreed to meet Rich's friend for coffee.

The appointed date and time rolled around, and those gal-lant thoughts were as wiped as I was by twelve hours of casting and watching auditions, followed by an important meeting about the film I was attempting to get off the ground. I would never make it out to the Coffee Bean & Tea Leaf in Venice on schedule, and I just didn't have the energy or time to give. I was scripting out my cancellation text in my head while chatting with my mom, and I mentioned it to her.

Mom disagreed. "Taylor, you should go. You gave him your word. You can really help him out and give this guy direction."

Mom was right. Mom knows best. I gathered up the very last of my energy and headed out to honor my word and live in service. I psyched myself up on the way over—maybe something good would come of this. Maybe something great. Maybe the stranger would be extraordinarily talented. Maybe he'd be lucky and get his breakthrough opportunity soon, and he'd kindly remember the exhausted lady who'd helped him prepare to nur-ture it. Sure, maybe I was just going to be true to myself, my word, and my service, which was more than enough in itself, but you never know—maybe this was my next breakthrough oppor-tunity in disguise.

I had no idea what the stranger looked like or even his full name, but as I walked across the street towards the coffee shop,

I recognized him right away. I'd seen this man before; I knew his eyes. They'd never been up on the silver screen, but I knew them as well as I knew my own. My heart skipped a beat as it recognized the breakthrough opportunity in front of me. This was the man I'd been praying for and dreaming of since I was eight years old. I didn't know his last name yet, but I knew someday we'd share it.

I apologized for being a few minutes late, and explained what I had been doing the past week and how long I'd been working on acting-related things that day. When David responded, "There is no way I could do that," I smiled. As I'd suspected, this stranger had no chance of becoming an actor. Even though I had not walked into the breakthrough acting opportunity of my life, I wasn't mad and I certainly didn't feel like I'd wasted any of my time or energy. I'd walked into the breakthrough love of my life. I couldn't have been happier.

It took several weeks of dating for David to admit that our first meeting had been a blind date—a complete setup. But I already knew the biggest breakthrough in my entire life didn't happen by accident. It wasn't just two random strangers meeting. David and Rich may have colluded, but there was more to it than just that. I had prayed and prepared myself to meet David for nearly twenty years, living in the service mode and using the gifts God gave me. And when that wasn't enough, when I almost canceled, I had the support and counsel of my mom. My suspicions were correct: this "stranger" was never committed to doing the work it takes to break through in acting. He was never interested in acting at all. But Mom was more right: I did give this guy direction . . . and he gave it to me. Now, we drive each day towards bigger and better breakthroughs, together.

David and I got married on June 23, 2019, and the first six months of our marriage were a flurry of breakthrough opportunities, personally and professionally. Though we were frequently on the road, even our "couch time" was productive. I'd wrapped up ABC's *The Fix* just before our wedding, so I prepared auditions for other even bigger roles; David sat beside me and wrote his first book, *Pivot & Go*. Knowing I was sharing top-foreword billing with Jeremy Lin, I poured everything into introducing my brilliant husband's debut book to the world.

When David asked me to write a foreword for this one, his second book, I cringed. What more could I talk about? Hadn't I covered everything David is to me in the first foreword? What could I possibly say about breakthroughs in early 2021? The pace of our life changed dramatically in 2020, along with the pace of the rest of the world. Suddenly, my production schedules were postponed and shifted; David's speaking engagements were called off. We were told to sit tight—worldwide all non-medical breakthroughs were postponed indefinitely, if not canceled altogether.

But while 2020 may have initially seemed like a slowdown in breakthrough opportunities, David and I actually found and created richer and deeper ones. David created virtual speaking engagements to inspire, motivate, and serve people across the globe dealing with uncertainty and fear, and he wrote another book; I found my head filled with original stories and characters I wanted to see on screen, and I dedicated myself to collaborating on scripts and pitching them to production companies and networks. We had time we never would have imagined to dedicate to our own growth, our growth together, and the growth of our team—including the addition of our puppy, Pivot. (Yes, he is named after the first book.) We had opportunities we could not have foreseen to act in service to our struggling communities. We had time to really reflect on our purpose.

Sitting on the couch with Pivot one night at the height of quarantine in September 2020, David turned to me and asked, "Am I the same person I was when I met you?"

I realized he wasn't the stranger I met at the Coffee Bean & Tea Leaf; he wasn't even the person I married the year before. Neither of us were. Though we will always be introducing ourselves to each other, and though we will always be soulmates, we are different now. We learn more and fall deeper in love with each other every day. Sure, I've fallen harder for him as we've traveled to amazing places together, but I've also fallen harder for him realizing he will never take the time to fold his clothes—that our dressers will always be stuffed with rolled-up jumbles. Of course I've loved sharing gourmet meals with him—even after realizing that I will never be able to take a bite before he films the entire spread on his phone. Sharing these daily joys, even the ones that drive me a little batty, is our key to turning our opportunities into wider breakthroughs—and we schedule them into our time. Every night before bed, we tell each other all the joys we had throughout the day and celebrate each other. No matter what amazing things God has blessed us with as individuals, we celebrate each other every day—on schedule. We are a breakthrough team, and we prioritize each other's growth—not when it's convenient to us, not once it's reached a breaking point, but as a natural part of our daily lives.

As David launches his second book, I see a person who is even more sure of who he is, more sure of the mission he is on, and a leader for not only our family, but for the world. I met a man who said he would do things; I married a man who actually did the things he said; I am a life partner to a man who makes things happen. Everyone is always perplexed with how he does it, but I've got the inside scoop: he uses this Breakthrough Blueprint, over and over, each day of his life. The formula in this book is the one my husband actually employs to make impossible things happen. It's the one I've now adopted to make impossible things happen. I'm so proud of him, I am so grateful for him, and I'm frankly astounded he's giving away the secrets to breakthrough success like this. David might be a mindset magician, but he's always been tapped into a truth that takes most of us longer to appreciate: we break through by helping others break through.

David stole my heart the day I met him. He won my heart the day I married him. He is on a daily pursuit to make me feel like the most special person in the world—a true breakthrough and the blueprint to our amazing marriage! But David is also a servant leader. He is so comfortable in his own skin that, at times, I have to tell him to tone it down in public. He makes random strangers feel like they have been best friends since elementary school; he can drain himself of all emotional energy because he is so concerned about helping everyone he talks to and fully pouring himself into them. I know I have to share him with the world (even when I don't always want to), because everyone deserves the blueprint to the daily joy in their lives, their careers, their relationships, and their futures that David has gifted to me.

The pages ahead are the biggest breakthrough opportunity you have ever been presented. I hope you use them to their fullest potential.

INTRODUCTION

You are the best of the best. It doesn't matter if you're the CEO of a Fortune 500 company or the parent of a toddler way overdue for a nap (or both!), you are the smartest, most talented, best-positioned individual to live exactly the life you were meant to live.

But being the best is a challenge. You've got less breathing room and fewer areas for incremental improvement. No matter what industry you're in, innovation is critical to your business operations. In rapidly changing environments, it's not enough to be the best. You can't rely on yesterday's performance; you need exponential growth and constant improvements. Your teams rely on you to do it smarter and better each day than the one before. We are all relying on your work, on your genius—on you—to have the next breakthrough that will revolutionize the way the job is done.

I'm not here to hand you your next breakthrough. You are the world's foremost expert in *you*—what you have accomplished, what you are capable of, and what you dream of doing. You're going to blow us all away with your breakthrough, and I can't wait!

No, literally—I can't keep waiting around for you to have a sudden jolt of inspiration, some happy accident that reshapes the world. So I'm going to teach you the system to build, schedule, and achieve your next breakthrough.

I've relied on breakthroughs throughout my career. Before I could even tie my own shoes, I was determined to make a name for myself in basketball. I set my heart on a game where the primary offensive focus was to get the ball to a dominant big man (aka Shaq) in the post and let them go to work. When I graduated college and started my professional basketball career, nearly every top draft pick was a seven-foot-tall giant with promising upside.

I was never going to be tall, fast, or athletic enough to achieve my dream. But I was still positive I could break through. I just needed to change the way the game was played.

There was one thing I could do on the court—shoot three-pointers. I watched my uncle, Nick Nurse, become one of the best three-point shooters in college basketball, and I grew up down the road from Kyle Korver, who would become one of the best three-point shooters in NBA history. I put in my 10,000 hours (and then some) developing my shot from beyond the arc. I was convinced three-point shooting was the future of the NBA.

The NBA disagreed. They treated three-point shots (really, any type of volume shooting) more like a party trick than a serious skill . . . until the seventh pick of the 2009 NBA draft came along. Steph Curry's scouting report was infamously weak: "Tweener, small frame, not explosive, bad shot selection." He was too short, too slow, and not nearly athletic enough—and those weren't the only things we had in common. Steph got out there and played his game, shooting threes. A lot of threes.

Overnight, the entire paradigm shifted. The big man quickly went the way of the dinosaur. Now, every single NBA player had to shoot threes. The NBA finally needed me as much as I'd always wanted them, because if there was one thing I did better than shooting, it was teaching others to shoot. After years of running shooting camps all over the world, living out of rental cars and airplane terminals, I became one of the top shooting coaches in the country and through an email in my junk box I nearly clicked 'delete' on, landed a spot with the Brooklyn Nets.

At first, I thought my breakthrough was lucky. Who am I to deserve this? Working with NBA players, though, I realized that my "luck" was a combination of factors—and that those factors were universal. Through in-depth trials (and a lot of errors), I pieced together the simple, tried-and-true, four-part formula that any athlete could employ to spark their own breakthrough. It worked flawlessly, turning elite performers into breakthrough impact optimization machines—what I call BIOnic leaders. Just as long as they committed to it.

But who has time for another commitment? Top athletes have nearly every millisecond of their day scheduled and planned—every bite they put in their mouths, every play they make, practice they do, sleep they get, everything. They couldn't choose between playing at their peak and working through the breakthrough formula. Breakthroughs and performing at the top had to work in unison. While I saw some incredible break-throughs from players able to commit to the formula, I knew I was missing an important piece—the piece would enable every BIOnic leader to lead a breakthrough day on and off the court.

As I searched for this important piece to make my formula truly universal, I became obsessed with what exactly makes an elite performer an elite performer. I was on the search for *greatness*. My business morphed as I did, from professional basketball player to NBA shooting coach to leadership motivation expert. It's an unusual background for corporate boardrooms, but the mindset and the systems I established in the NBA outshine any I learned in my MBA. In all my consulting work, I've yet to find a business challenge, leadership initiative, or mental training that didn't have a direct parallel in basketball. No matter where I've gone or who I've coached, the breakthrough formula worked—but no elite per-former had the precious time to spend on the treasure hunt.

Even in my own life, the notion of a bad quarter seemed like a luxury—one lousy week could have (and sometimes did!) ruin my business's reputation, kill any hard-won momentum, and financially destroy my shareholders (aka me). Staying competi-tive meant constantly innovating—doing it better and smarter than my competition and than myself the day before. In order to integrate the formula into my own life, I needed a structure. I needed to be able to schedule my breakthroughs, to actually stick them in my calendar.

To conquer the complicated, we must first bring it back to the simple. I deconstructed my own formula and everything I knew about breakthroughs, and started beta testing new systems. When I started quickly, painlessly, even joyfully delivering breakthroughs on a rapid-fire schedule, I knew I had the perfect formula anyone could use to become a BIOnic leader.

The formula is failproof and infinitely scalable. It will not consume your time, energy, money, or any other resources. This book explains the seamless system, and walks you through the process of building your own breakthroughs. You'll be given the questions and tools you need, as well as examples of these breakthrough components in action. Strong emphasis on the word *action*. Our brains are filled on a daily basis with knowledge from nearly every media medium on the planet. Sure, we *know*, but how many of us actually *do*? You're the only one who can take action and apply it to your own life, and it won't be easy. You'll have to challenge your own "best practices" and learn more about yourself, your team, your world, and your purpose. You'll need to pivot your approach, your perspective, and the ways you measure your success. You'll need to tap into every resource you have. I can show you how to think differently, but you're the only one who can *do differently*.

Living the breakthrough mode doesn't necessarily make any of the challenges you're facing any easier, but it does make tackling every one of them fulfilling. I'm positive you can do it. I've been incredibly fortunate to live and work in spaces where I see breakthroughs—game-changing, world-altering breakthroughs at the highest level of human performance—happen every day. I've learned from the best of the best getting better, and I'm here to guide you along your beautiful journey. We'll warm up with the Breakthrough Impact Optimization (BIOnic) Tools you need to embrace, then we'll launch into the most important questions—the who, what, where, and why—that are standing between you and your greatest breakthrough. By integrating finding answers to those into your day, you'll organically conquer the "when," scheduling your breakthroughs right into your day, no matter what roadblock you're facing.

No more hoping and wishing and waiting. It's time to take action and become the breakthrough!

CHAPTER 1

Warm Up: The Breakthrough Formula

Between playing professional basketball, winning two Guinness World Records, training a few hundred NBA clients, and coaching so many basketball camps across the globe that I've literally lost count, I've earned a reputation as one of the best shooters and shooting coaches in the world. Trust me—I can tell the difference between a good player and a breakthrough performer before we even step on the court. If you want to do differently, you have to prepare differently.

That's something we've all internalized already, right? You stretch your hamstrings before you hit the pavement for a grueling run. You rinse your scuba mask and clear your lungs before you dive into the chilly depths. You lift lighter before you work your way up to your one-rep max. Before you jump into anything strenuous, you warm up.

Yet when you're hunting intangible, elusive, innovation-critical breakthroughs, you throw every warm-up out the window and think they're just going to appear. You jump right into the game and start throwing desperate half-court Hail Mary heave-shots before you even lace up your shoes. It's purely accidental if you hit any of them. More often than not, you just end up depleting yourself and your team of all the energy you need to pump into bringing your breakthroughs to life. It's no mystery why the topic of recovery is just as hot in the corporate world as it is in athletics—we're all burning ourselves out.

You don't want to just have breakthroughs; you want to lead breakthrough days that sustain and boost you (and, of course, the people and projects you care about). You can't get there by doing things the way you've always done them. Status quo is great for just getting by—you need to break through!

Elite athletes wear the evidence of their physical training right out in the open; what's hidden are the equal amounts of mindset training they do. Forget the bulging biceps and the powerful quads; if you could look inside their heads, you'd see the true breakthrough muscle—their brains. No amount of practice and physical finetuning matters if your mind isn't in shape and ready to take on the day.

Athletes constantly train their mind-body connections. The best NBA players warm up for shooting by connecting to *everything*—the feel of the ball, the sounds of the court, the blood pumping through their veins. They ignite every one of their senses, because they know they need to bring it all into the game. They make their intangible breakthroughs tactile before they even start playing.

When I started bringing my mindset training into corporations, I was shocked to find cultures with so little emphasis on this crucial mind-body connection. Sure, many of these elite leaders worked out and ate well, but when they hit the office, they were trying to break through their challenges with brain brute force. Not happening.

Have you ever heard that we only use 10 percent of our brains? People who study MRIs swear that isn't true, but I'm pretty sure it actually is—at least the way most of us operate. Even if all your synapses are firing, if you're not working your brain in concert with your body and all your sensory input, you're only achieving a small portion of your potential. Compartmentalizing your brain from your body and your environment blocks off at least 90 percent of your available breakthroughs!

Most people are taught to think *around* their senses, but every portion of the Breakthrough Blueprint includes connecting *with* your senses. Training your brain to soak up all the sensory information you've been leaving on the table can be uncomfortable at first, but it's essential. Bring that wasted 90 percent into your breakthrough efforts—start with making your warm-up tangible.

When Aristotle ranked our senses, he argued that touch was the least important; I'm here to tell you that Aristotle would have been a *terrible* shooter. I doubt he even would have been the breakthrough genius we still talk about today if he hadn't spent so much time in Plato's gym! The things we can touch, our tangibles, are what we trust most. To warm up for your breakthrough day and get into the BIOnic (Breakthrough Impact Optimization) mindset, you need to dominate your SENSE:

Stop Solving Problems.

Eliminate Goals.

Navigate the How.

Seize the Formula.

Embrace the Clock.

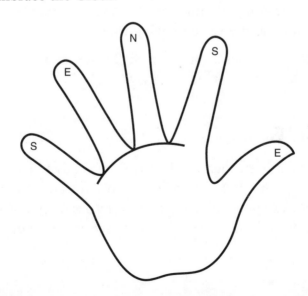

These five concepts are the keys to your Breakthrough Blueprint. They're simple, but they're also pretty radical shifts from business-as-usual. Warm up by getting a sense of SENSE.

STOP SOLVING PROBLEMS

From the court to the boardroom, elite performers are always excited to learn new skills. As a coach, the toughest lessons to teach aren't the things you need to start doing, but what you need to *stop* doing. It doesn't matter how many awesome skills you learn if you don't quit your worst habits.

This is a big one.

Brainstorming solutions is very tempting. Get a little bit creative to address simple challenges, and you walk away feeling good—but you're rarely tackling the underlying issue. If you think about it, the human body is like a case study on the futility of solving problems. If your hip hurts, your hip probably isn't the problem—it's your hamstring or your quad, it's your desk chair or the way you carry your wallet. Everything is connected. You might be able to solve the hip pain with a quick cortisol shot, but that's only a temporary fix. Until you understand the connections, you're just resolving symptoms.

Take a step back from your challenges, and stop trying to solve problems. Your breakthrough is bigger!

ELIMINATE GOALS

Your drive has been channeled into setting goals and doing whatever it takes to hit them. Who doesn't love the endorphin rush of winning a championship ring, hitting a sales quota, or securing that full ride college scholarship? Let's see some results!

But is securing your goal actually a breakthrough? Are you even sure that you're the one who chose your goals? If you understood more about your larger mission, would you still choose the goal you've set?

When I hear goals like "make a billion dollars," "shoot the most three-pointers in the league this season," or "play a sold-out stadium tour," I want to know what's driving them. The more obvious and desirable the goals ("David, who wouldn't want that?"), the more I worry about the breakthrough potential. If you want to create something the world has never seen, you need to think differently *and* do differently.

Learn more about your mission; get a sense of your breakthrough purpose. Your goals should be serving your breakthrough—useful and actionable guides to the results you alone can reach. Your breakthroughs will be as unique as you are; starting off with goals is like slipping on blinders that keep you narrowly focused on something mediocre that many could achieve, or it leaves you with a target too broad and ineffectual to really innovate on.

NAVIGATE THE HOW

Every breakthrough—big or small, personal or professional—centers on answering a "how" question.

Once an elite performer recognizes that the key to breakthrough results is answering the right "how," you scramble to find your "how." Unfortunately, that's a really lousy instinct.

You deserve incredible, innovative, and unique solutions to questions like:

- How can we outperform our highest aspirations?
- How do we make our relationships more loving?
- How do we keep production, motivation, and drive high?

- How do we prioritize everything we need to accomplish in a day?

- How do we distinguish ourselves from our competition in a disruptive 24/7 environment?

- How do we heal from the hardest blows in life?

- How do we pivot every challenge into something actionable and collaborative?

- How do we constantly and consistently come up with creative, life-altering ideas and follow through on them?

But if you want answers to these, you need to create the conditions in which breakthroughs not only can happen, but can come to life. You don't get that by chasing "how"—you get that by finding answers to the who, what, where, and why of the breakthrough formula. System + Process = Results. Follow the system in the formula through your daily process, and you'll get better "how" results than you can even imagine.

SEIZE THE FORMULA

Confidence + Cooperation + Service + Purpose

That's it. That's the breakthrough formula. But these four ingredients in the formula aren't what you think they are, nor what the world says they are. You'll see, you will have a paradigm shift, but trust me: this shift will be exactly what you have been searching for. If you are confident, cooperative, acting in service, and have a sense of purpose, you are already in the process of breaking through. You are living in the space where breakthroughs occur naturally and easily. If you're not already experiencing a constant string of breakthroughs each and every day, you act on the formula by tackling these big four questions:

Breakthrough Confidence: **Who** are you?

Breakthrough Cooperation: **What** relationships matter?

Breakthrough Service: **Where** are you helping?

Breakthrough Purpose: **Why** are you playing?

Everyone has breakthrough ideas; a rare few act on them; a *very* rare few build lives where their breakthrough ideas can immediately come to life. This formula is the system you need to drive actual results from your amazing ideas. Don't scramble to answer these questions now (we're going to build out the details together throughout the entirety of the book); just commit to the formula and get pumped about being one of the very rare.

EMBRACE THE CLOCK

Developing your breakthroughs through who, what, where, and why sounds great, but *when?* When are you going to have time for all that?!

Once you stop fighting the clock, there's actually no better tool to support your breakthrough.

The breakthrough formula is a four-quadrant schedule that overlays your day so you can have, perform, *and* achieve at breakthrough levels, all at the same time. It doesn't require you to change anything about your schedule. You become a perpetual breakthrough machine!

It doesn't require you to reschedule anything. The tools and perspective pivots you'll practice each quarter can be done while you commute, take meetings, spend time with your friends and family, and accomplish everything you need to get done. All it requires up front is a commitment to shifting your over-arching focus four times over the course of each day.

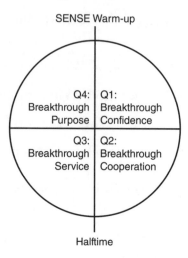

SENSE Warm-up

Q4:
Breakthrough
Purpose

Q1:
Breakthrough
Confidence

Q3:
Breakthrough
Service

Q2:
Breakthrough
Cooperation

Halftime

If you change absolutely nothing about your daily life besides reframing it into these quarters, the process will organically create breakthroughs. It couldn't be simpler: take the rough number of waking hours in your day, and divide by four. If you get eight hours of sleep each night, your breakthrough day is sixteen hours long. Each of your quarters will be four hours long. Say you wake up at six and start Q1; your Q2 will start at ten, Q3 at two, Q4 at six. Rotate through this schedule, complete the assigned tools each quarter, and engage your subconscious mind with that quarter's question while you do everything you would normally do, and you'll have an amazing day—regardless of what's on your calendar. You'll create an environment where your "how" can reveal itself, and it will be something that you can actually follow through on, something that you will enjoy and be stimulated by. The search for your answers becomes powerful and exciting, not stressed and miserable.

***

SENSE is a great warm-up for your breakthrough—*if you use it.*

This blueprint is exactly as effective as you make it. Reading the book will teach you how to think differently, but until you put the system into action, it won't have any impact on your breakthrough results.

Don't wait until you understand every word perfectly—practice is essential to getting even proficient. Don't even wait until you're finished the book. Start here; start now. There's no "someday" on the calendar. You're warmed up—so get out there and play. Today should be your breakthrough day!

WARM-UP TOOL: SNAP

No matter how committed you are to your breakthrough when you start your day, old patterns die hard. Breakthroughs aren't easy, or everyone would be having them. Whenever you find yourself veering back down the well-beaten path to mediocrity, SNAP back!

Equipment Required: Your Hand

Space Required: Anywhere

Time Required: <2 Minutes

Instructions:

1. When you feel disconnected from your breakthrough mission, physically snap your fingers as a cue to pivot back, and:

   - **S**top: Whatever you're doing—solving problems, feeling listless, losing motivation, or trying to brute force your breakthrough—physically and mentally throw on the brakes.

- **Notice:** Take note of what threw you out of the Breakthrough Blueprint. What is the roadblock? How frequently are you running into this problem, and what causes it?

- **Assess:** What do you need to get over this and back into the process? Take a breather, choose your second, and . . .

- **Pivot:** Turn back to the breakthrough formula with new strength and determination, and get back into your quarter—breakthrough confidence, cooperation, service, and purpose.

2. Keep your hands on the ready and don't disconnect from yourself; really let your breakthrough mindset impact everything you touch. The power to SNAP yourself back into your breakthrough is at your fingertips!

CHAPTER 2

Q1: Hearing Who: Breakthrough Confidence

Dedicate the first quarter of your breakthrough day to answering the pivotal "who"—who are you?

A singular breakthrough idea can come from just about anywhere. The foundation for living the blueprint, however, is breakthrough confidence.

Most people, certainly most elite performers, believe they are confident. You can look over your résumé and accomplishments with pride. You can move through this world with a good deal of swagger and certainty, which are invaluable for driving incredible results.

But do you have *breakthrough* confidence?

I have spent years surrounded by athletes in their late teens and early twenties who've been told they are the most talented players in the world—young men who have been promised unbelievable wealth for their skills, who draw the attention of celebrities and reporters and fans across the globe. The swagger that gives them is an essential element for being stars on NBA courts and for winning games.

But if they want to build truly breakthrough careers, they have to pivot their swagger into a very specific type of confident self-awareness. They have to maintain their pride in what they've accomplished and the talents they have spent countless hours cultivating, but they also need to dig into the parts of themselves they've buried. They need constructive ways to face the fears that they—and all confident people—expend a lot of energy avoiding and denying. They need the breakthrough confidence that gives them the grace and faith to ditch many things they're good at in order to focus on the things they're great at, to question their "flawed" attributes, to demand entry to the next level. They need the breakthrough confidence that transcends other's expectations, that accepts fear and identifies opportunities.

You can perform at high levels with confidence, but you can create entire universes with *breakthrough* confidence. It's the awareness that the way you perform is really the tip of the iceberg—the part you can see. Hate to break it to you, but your vision is blurry. It's easily tricked. Your eyes lie—a lot.

As a true child of the '90s, I spent my fair share of time with *Magic Eye* posters. Remember those? You stare at these incomprehensible swirls until everything resolves into a ship or a cat or whatever. And then you can't unsee it!

Humans have been creating visual illusions since we started dabbing colors on cave walls. We love to convince ourselves that we can control and shape reality, and the fact that our eyes are so eager to play along? Awesome!

But if you want breakthrough confidence, you're going to have to paint it by ear.

Your ears are honest, specifically designed to cut through the BS of the world. Did you know there are no auditory illusions in nature? Your ears can't play tricks on you like your eyes do. They work faster than your eyes. They're dialed in to sense changes almost instantly—like, in a microsecond. And they tune out nonessentials 24/7. Your hearing—not your vision, your thoughts, your résumé, or the opinions of the world around you—is your key to breakthrough confidence. As long as you don't lie to your ears, you have a perfect sensory partner for this quarter.

Breakthrough confidence starts with hearing about who you are. You aren't the things you've done—which is a comfort for some, but terrifying for many elite performers. Pride in your past accomplishments can become a crutch. Breakthrough confidence requires really digging into what you have hidden and what you fear. You have to ask yourself some tough questions, and really *listen* to the answers. Hearing how your answers change as you expand your breakthrough confidence is fundamental to your breakthrough.

Breakthrough confidence has to radiate from you; you cannot be given it, you cannot fake it, you cannot take anyone else's word for it. Hear about yourself from the greatest expert on Earth—you.

WHO ARE YOU HIDING?

Why would anyone as fabulous and talented as you need to hide anything?

Yet you're still hiding someone.

No judgments here. I've yet to meet an elite performer (myself included) who isn't hiding versions of themselves from the world. None of us can embrace and develop every talent we have simultaneously; we all have multiple versions of ourselves waiting on the bench. Choosing which version to develop is so tough that most people never really do. BIOnic leaders recognize that the urge not to choose, to stay stuck in neutral, waiting on the day when one of your hidden versions is perfect, is a decision in itself—the wrong one.

At some point, maybe soon—maybe even today—you're going to have to bring your next version out of hiding. You should know who you're dealing with.

***

When I was seven, a family moved in down the street who put the Cleavers to shame. The Korvers weren't just picture perfect—they were the most generous, caring, kind people you've ever met. Their door was always open, as was the concrete basketball court in their backyard.

Their oldest son, Kyle, was five years ahead of me and everything I wanted to be. He was a great student, beloved by everyone, and the best basketball player in town. This kid could do *everything*. When he came to one of my eighth-grade games and told me I'd be a great player someday, he earned a fan for life.

Kyle was the star of the Fighting Dutch, Pella High's basketball team, and I went to the games every Friday night to cheer them on. The team meant so much to me that my mom even let me skip school when Kyle led Pella to the state tournament in Des Moines his senior year. From a courtside seat at "The Barn," I had every opportunity to admire Kyle's game. He had a talent for shooting three-pointers, but he played with the confidence and the utility of a Swiss Army knife—handling the ball, being a playmaker, getting others open, and crashing the offensive boards. And he was good at all of it.

Truthfully, though, Kyle wasn't *great* at any of it, and the college scouts didn't share my fierce admiration for him. He didn't receive any D1 offers until Creighton University picked him up at the confidence-shaking twenty-fifth hour. Kyle psyched himself back up and stepped on the Omaha court for his first Blue Jay practice ready do it all, just like he had in high school.

All that confidence went right back out the door. Great athletes ran circles around him, better defenders stole the ball from him, skilled rebounders boxed him out—and these were his teammates, not his competition. Kyle just couldn't cut it.

Coach Dana Altman dropped some no-nonsense, ice cold reality: "The only way you are getting on the court is if you focus on three-point shooting. And nothing else. I didn't bring you here to dribble, I didn't bring you here to rebound. I brought you here to shoot threes. That's all I want you thinking about. Morning, afternoon, evening, shoot threes. Become the best damn three-point shooter in the country!"

Brash, yes, but it was exactly what Kyle needed—the direction and permission to focus on one thing and one thing only, to develop one of his many talents into an actual elite strength.

Kyle got obsessive about the number of three-pointers he shot. He didn't work a single other skill. And he became *outstanding*—one of the best three-point shooters in college basketball. The Philadelphia 76ers even chose him in the second round of the NBA draft after his senior season. While most second-round picks have two-year careers and never actually see the court, Kyle kept sharpening his three-pointers with breakthrough confidence. Over his now seventeen-season NBA career, he's made his elite strength one of the deadliest weapons in basketball.

As a kid, I admired Kyle Korver for being a high-level performer who could do it all. But watching him uncover the truly elite performer underneath changed my perspective. I no longer wanted to be the guy who did it all. I wanted to be the *best* in the world at one thing.

We are all born with various levels of aptitude in many things; we discover these gifts when we start crafting them into skills. Some kids start showing off amazing gifts before they're even fully potty trained. The three-year-old with perfect pitch has a leg up in music, just like the one who can dribble a soccer ball has a real shot at dominating the peewee team. That's not to say that every prodigy will take it to the next level, or that those with less natural aptitude won't surpass them. Choosing which of our gifts to specialize in and develop into elite strengths is a huge factor.

I think about the progression from aptitude to elite strength like making a smoothie. We all start off with a lot of ingredients, but in different amounts. I might have ten blueberries, half a banana, and an orange in my kitchen, while you might find twenty blueberries, an orange, and a bag of spinach in yours. You've got more blueberries, but if you dump all your ingredients in the blender, you could end up with mostly spinach flavor. If I concentrate on ripening my berries perfectly and leave the orange out, I could end up with a *way* better blueberry smoothie.

No matter how much natural aptitude you have, developing it into an elite strength is a choice. If you have a lot of natural aptitude for many skills, choosing which one to develop can seem pointless. Before Kyle went to college, I doubt he even knew he was hiding an elite strength. Who would have told him? We admire well-rounded people, high-level performers who can do it all. We're told not to put all our eggs in one basket.

But that's what elite strength requires. No one is *the best* at everything. Doing a lot of things mediocre-to-good is hiding. Kyle was hiding his potential as an elite performer because everyone supported his well-rounded high performance. When he went to the next level, his good-enough wasn't good enough. He had to choose to bring out another version of himself—Kyle Korver, three-point champion.

Kyle's breakthrough never would have happened if he'd insisted on staying the hometown basketball Swiss Army knife. Trust me, I have done a lot of workouts with Kyle. He dribbles off his foot for about thirty seconds before dedicating himself to his world-class strength. I've seen him make fifty-three straight threes on the move after two hours of shooting on the last drill of the last workout of the week.

Breakthrough confidence requires focusing on your elite strength and refusing to be well-rounded into a bunch of mediocre skills. High performers might have the natural aptitude to do it all well, but it's bad time and energy management. You're hiding someone important for your breakthrough, and you're not giving your best to yourself or anyone else. From athletics to business to parenting, "It takes a village" doesn't mean that every person needs to fill the same twenty roles. Have the breakthrough confidence to be your strength, so you can work with integrity in breakthrough cooperation with other elite performers for truly spectacular results.

Who is the elite performer you're hiding behind the person doing it all?

***

When my friend Boris Kodjoe accepted a tennis scholarship at Virginia Commonwealth University, everyone already knew he was destined for greatness. His entire childhood in Germany had been devoted to the tennis courts, and he was determined to make his mark on the professional circuit, so he packed his bags and flew to the U.S. with the future of the sport riding on his shoulders.

That weight was too much. At the age of seventeen, Boris injured his back—and learned he had congenital stenosis (a narrow spinal canal). This pinching sciatic nerve would eventually just become chronic pain. The doctors basically told him he might as well go back to Germany and start working for the local pub, because that's where his future was headed.

Boris didn't know what to do, where to turn, or whom to reach out to for help. His inner cry was muffled by the fact that he knew just enough English to say hello and order a hamburger. Life had let him down; there was no chance his elite strength would take him anywhere.

Boris decided to stick it out and hope for a miracle. He played tennis all through college, continuing to develop the elite strength he'd dedicated his life to. But no miracle arrived.

Boris and his brother Patrick (who came to VCU on a basketball scholarship) took a road trip up to New York City in the spring of 1995. They were just walking along when a man accosted Boris based on his appearance. Sadly, that wasn't a new experience for the brothers. Their mother is Austrian and their father is Ghanaian, and they'd grown up as the only black children in town; they were used to being bullied and ostracized for looking different.

But they'd never gotten a reaction like this one. The tall, slender, fashionable man abruptly demanded Boris become a model and handed him a business card. Ford Modeling.

Boris hesitated—he was an athlete, not a model. He'd considered his appearance a flaw his entire life. But Patrick pushed him to check it out. Within months, Boris became one of the most recognizable faces in male modeling. The smooth, melanin-rich skin that had once made him an outcast now graced billboards throughout the world. The feature that he'd been tormented for was, in fact, an attribute that brought him closer to a breakthrough.

Falling asleep to the glow of his small black and white TV as a child, he had often dreamt of the bright lights of Hollywood. Having a recognizable face is obviously a huge asset for breaking into films, and after Boris was featured in the TLC music video for "Red Light Special," everyone knew him. He was ready for the big screen!

Casting directors disagreed; Boris's strong German accent and limited English fluency were big hurdles. He began putting the energy, time commitment, work ethic, relentless consistency, and daily drive he'd previously dedicated to tennis into his acting skills. Photo shoot after photo shoot, Boris practiced his English vocabulary and accent work. Five years and well over 10,000 hours later, Boris was the breakthrough star of *Love & Basketball*, and the rest is history. Over the past twenty years, Boris has become one of the top actors in Hollywood and expanded his skills into producing, writing, and directing.

Boris was born with incredible athletic aptitude; with encouragement, he developed it into an elite strength at a very young age. However, Boris's elite tennis strength had a shelf life—all elite strengths do.

Even if you dedicate your entire life to developing one attribute and become the absolute best in the world, that elite strength will not carry you through every breakthrough. Sooner or later, everyone reaches the failure point of their most developed strength. Boris just hit his earlier than most.

This can bust anyone's confidence, particularly professional athletes, but I've seen it in every field. Many clients concentrate so much time and energy into developing their elite strength that they no longer recognize their adjacent skills. They're watching all their dreams go up in smoke, questioning who they are without their elite strength, and trying to build up the courage to develop another from scratch.

I wish elite strengths came with the shelf life clearly stamped, like milk cartons. It would set expectations and help with this incredible sense of loss. From one elite performer who has been through it: don't despair. You're not starting from scratch— nowhere near. In developing that now-failed elite strength, you developed other skills and attributes to near elite levels. More importantly, you learned *how* to develop an elite strength. You're not the same person anymore—but you're so close to finding the person you need now, someone you've been hiding.

Look more closely at your "flaws" to discover your most unique elite strengths—the "weird" attributes you were punished for, taught to feel ashamed of, and told to hide. Those attributes made you *different*. Different scares people. Disruption scares people. Breakthroughs scare the crap out of people. You weren't encouraged to develop your skills in these areas. But embracing them now, with determination and drive? That's breakthrough confidence. You're refusing to keep hiding someone the world considered flawed, and examining the most unique attributes you can bring to breakthroughs.

Boris was born with athletic talent that earned him praise and a complexion that people ridiculed, but both of these attributes were God-given, even when no one recognized it. He honed more than one skill as he developed his tennis game. He embraced the mindset and methods to develop *any* elite strength. Every time Boris and I meet up, I can count on two things: 1) We'll end up eating too much at Tocaya Organica; and 2) he'll say, "David, I don't think there is any skill that I can't master. I truly don't. I believe we all have a gift, and it's our duty to find out what is. And when we do, we must use it for the betterment of the world we live in." That's breakthrough confidence on every level.

Boris's first elite strength was just a setup for something greater. We often think the elite strength we currently possess is our ultimate strength; in reality, it might just lead us to the next unique strength. When immense setbacks occur, accept the light they shine on attributes you've buried. Refusing to examine your "flaws" is hiding someone capable of a breakthrough that can shake up the entire world.

When you hide the version of yourself that disturbs ignorant people, you end up accepting that their judgment is real—that your unique attributes are "flaws." I meet confident, formerly bullied people incapable of laughing at themselves and their mistakes, unwilling to embrace their quirkiness, unable to comfort the people they mentor, from their co-workers to their children. I even meet confident people who, actively or passively, bully people themselves. Who are you most afraid your kid will be?

What do you make people feel ashamed about? What does that tell you about the "flaws" you're hiding from yourself?

When you reach the failure point of your elite strength, you absolutely have a high-level skill waiting to level up. If you are having trouble finding it, look at the activities you are driven towards that others find inconsequential, weird, or even grotesque. If you spend every available hour playing video games, you have a skill. You are an elite strategist in training. If you're a drug runner, you have a skill. With a small pivot, you are an elite business developer and operations guru. If you go to the same dead-end job every day with regret and expectations weighing on you, you have a skill. You are an elite pain overcomer. You have been through hell, and now you can coach others through your pain experience. Even NBA players and CEOs who have reached the shelf life of their current strengths are just beginning to scratch the surface of who they can be and are going to be!

Who are you hiding because the world labeled them flawed?

WHO ARE YOU FOOLING?

Really? *No one?* Why the heck not?

Confident people walk into situations knowing they are fully qualified and have everything on lock. They are the smartest, most elite performers in the room, and they are here to deliver the goods. They are absolutely *not* imposters.

Breakthrough confidence requires stress-testing the next level—walking into the rooms you are *not* qualified for. You have to put yourself in make-or-break situations to develop your elite strengths to higher levels and determine your adjacent skills. Identify the next level you can take your elite strength to by playing like the elite performer your résumé *says* you are. Forget imposter syndrome—breakthrough confidence means becoming an actual imposter.

***

By the time they knocked on my door, the gorgeous Japanese hotel room seemed like a cage. My time was up. Practice was starting, and I was about to be unmasked as an imposter.

I was twenty-five when I pitched myself as the official consultant to Okinawa, Japan's Golden Kings basketball team. I could advise the GM on constructing the team, advise the coaches on running offense and defense, and advise the players on improving their individual games. It all seemed so simple when I was sitting stateside, beefing up my résumé and vying for the job. Sure, maybe I hadn't done anything *exactly* like this before (nothing close to it), but I was confident and talented. Anything I wasn't skilled in yet would come easy if they did pick me, right?

Sitting in a foreign country listening to people rapidly throw out questions I didn't know the answers to in a language I wasn't fluent in was a whole different game. I didn't know how a team was supposed to be run; I had only watched others do it, only studied the intricacies of culture and chemistry from the outside. I had no idea how to actually *do* it.

I marched to my execution—the first basketball practice— and entered the gym knowing I had nothing on my side. No hard skills to roll out. No gift of gab could transcend the awkward translation process. In a culture where age equals wisdom and authority, I was twenty-five and looked twenty. Every person on that floor and in the organization was older than me. Even the water boy.

I ran to the coaches' room to unmask myself before someone else did it for me. I could salvage at least a little honor by explaining what I was *actually* capable of doing for the team, right?

Then I ran into a more intimidating figure than my worst nightmares—a real Japanese samurai warrior.

It took me a moment to realize that this samurai was a life-sized, fully armored statue. I was alone in the room. I stared at the statue in wonder—though I was no scholar, I'd been fascinated by the legends of these fearless warriors since I was a kid. They spent their whole lives training; they were given toy swords when they were just three years old, and progressed from training to practice, and finally, to battle. When I was three, I wasn't training for anything except a full-time gig out of diapers—well, and basketball. I was already dedicated to my toy basketball, for sure.

I laughed, recognizing the sign God was giving me. Like the samurai, I had been training for this moment since I could crawl. It was time to step up to the challenge. The samurai wouldn't run out and announce this was his first battle—he made everyone fear the skills he had built over so many years. This was my chance to live with the same honor.

That first day was a blur, as were the following thirteen. I'm pretty sure I made up half of the questions I answered directly on the spot, but I did so with courage and the command I'd been training to take my entire life. That's not to say I intuited every trick of the trade on my first round; I was forced to grow on the spot. I learned more about myself and the game of basketball by walking through the fire than I had through years of study. I leaned on my high-level offensive strengths and on my brothers in battle, the American import players, to help me with defensive alignment and rotations.

I took my coaching game to the next level, and Okinawa went on to make the playoffs. A two-week consultation job turned into many more, and at the end of our third year, we won the Japanese championship. A team that hadn't existed before I'd gotten involved now sat at the highest pinnacle of the sport.

I'd truly earned the honors I'd claimed on my original résumé, and then some.

I have since been called to Japan and fifty other countries to consult and share my expertise on building teams, coaching, and developing players. And none of that would have happened if I hadn't *lied my butt off* the first time—and performed up to my fullest "reach" potential.

Is your résumé scrupulously accurate—or does it depict the elite strengths you *will* have? Make a new résumé that lays claim to every skill you are positive you could develop if given the opportunity. Whether you actually can develop it or it becomes a primary focus of your complements wish list, it might be just the skill your breakthrough is crying out for. Embrace the imposter within you!

No matter how elite you are, there is some part of you waiting for the permission to play at the next level. The magical allure of that next rung on the ladder: that's when you can *really* be who you were made to be. Screw that. Steal it. Breakthrough confidence doesn't wait.

Volunteer to take on a project you know will make you uncomfortable; don't tell anyone that you're brand-new and way out of your wheelhouse. If you have never done an in-person presentation, *do that*! If you have never fired someone, do that! If you are feeling imposter syndrome in any part of your life, embrace it! There is something next-level that scares you. That's meaningful. Do it.

Who does your imposter résumé say you're going to become today?

***

Until you demand entry to the *next level*, you won't get there—and you won't earn the interest and respect of the people who can help you reach it. Even if (especially if!) people realize you're not supposed to be there, your elite strength and breakthrough confidence should have them questioning why.

My head wasn't the only one that turned when a sixteen-year-old walked into the St. Monica's gym. From September through May, he'd be right at home on these high school courts, but it was a sweltering hot July afternoon in Santa Monica, and he was in a whole different universe.

From June through August, the St. Monica gym is one of the most exclusive invites in the country. The only people allowed in are high-level NBA execs, Wasserman agents, the best of the best NBA players, and their trainers. Had the agent walking in with this kid pulled every string and risked his career just to let him watch the workouts?

When the kid laced up to hit the courts, I figured the agent was about to get fired. My eyes widened as I was instructed to include him in the game, but I went along with it. You don't work for long in basketball without recognizing that the agent is *always* right. This child was about to go head-to-head against some of the top NBA All-Stars. He was going to be obliterated.

As I picked teams to evenly distribute the immense talent, I stuck the kid on reserve. Maybe he would get a minute or two on court; nothing that would affect the flow of the game or piss off the NBA players there to sharpen their skills exclusively against the cream of the crop.

The game started with all of the intensity of a playoff Game 7. When All-Stars play just for bragging rights, the games often overshadow the real season. Pride among peers means everything to NBA players—as it does to all elite performers. We don't just want to be one of the best; we want to be *the* best.

Midway through the first game, the high school kid checked in, stepping onto the floor with players who held over a billion dollars' worth of NBA contracts, and I braced myself for a crash. To my relief, he actually managed to get into the flow pretty quickly.

As he ran up the sidelines in transition, I saw his eyes light up. The ball was suddenly in his hands, and with one defender on the perimeter and one awaiting him at the hoop, he exploded downhill with his eyes set on the rim.

There was no way he was going to attempt a dunk—right?

In slow-motion beauty, the kid took off from outside of the lane and rose . . . and continued to rise . . . and as if he was defying gravity itself, he rose even higher still. With an explosive sound, he ripped down the rim with a force so violent, you would have thought someone had just stolen his little brother's lunch money.

This kid had just dunked on two defenders—two NBA superstars—at the same time. It was unreal. I stood there rubbing my eyes like a baffled cartoon character while the kid trotted back on defense like it was just another day at the office.

I turned to the agent and whispered, "Who is that guy?"

"Anthony Edwards," he responded with a smile. "He's only a junior, but he's already the top high school player in the country. Surefire lock to be the number one draft pick when he's eligible."

You've most likely heard his name by now. The agent was right; Edwards was the first pick in the first round of the 2020 NBA draft. He's already distinguished himself in his rookie year as the third-youngest player to score more than 40 points in a single game—trailing only LeBron James and Kevin Durant. Anthony Edwards is destined to be one of the NBA GOATs.

In July 2018, Anthony Edwards had none of the qualifications and bona fides to be in the gym at St. Monica's, much less on the floor—except that this was a space for the future of the

NBA, and he knew he *was* the future of the NBA. He had break-through confidence in his talent and the impact he was going to have on the sport, and he made it felt.

Breakthrough confidence is demanding entry to the rooms you deserve to be in based on the strength of your unacknowl-edged talent—not on any preexisting consensus. You have the ability, the drive, and the self-awareness—so why are you waiting for someone else to decide that you've proven yourself? It's a waste of your time, and it keeps you from playing on the level you're meant to be. Question all the stated and unstated require-ments to exclusive clubs, and define your own peer group—even if they don't know you're on their level yet. *Especially* if they don't know you're on their level yet! Ask questions at meetings you're not "senior" enough to even attend. Crash parties, make calls. Create your own experience; take the reins into your own hands.

If you are only standing in rooms that fully accept you, you are not operating with breakthrough confidence. I can't count the number of times I have stepped into a boardroom to moti-vate people twice my age and ten times my net worth, knowing that I needed to jump the hurdle of their judgment before I could even prove my value. It's made me a much stronger speaker than if I had insisted on staying in my lane.

Whose court are you going to play on today?

WHO CAN EAT YOU ALIVE?

No one, right?

Confidence is control. You've got a plan for that. Or you'll figure it out when you get there. With your elite skills and strengths, no one can possibly eat you alive. Sure, some apex predator might come at you, but you are supremely confident in your top product—yourself. There is no person, place, or thing you can't make that sale to. If they're not buying, you're confident you can tweak the offering, shift the pitch, even level yourself up. No one can, or would even want to eat you—you're more valuable to them working towards your next breakthrough.

That's incompetent confidence.

Breakthrough confidence recognizes you haven't developed these elite skills to sell—you have developed them as important tools to serve and change the world. Your breakthrough isn't for sale, and it will happen regardless of how much buy-in you have from the people around you. Breakthrough confidence embraces that no amount of preparation, research, development, or control will keep someone from eating you alive. There is no strength so elite and developed that it can control all the variables.

Breakthrough confidence is knowing with absolute certainty that you will get eaten alive. We all will. The real question isn't how to avoid it—it's whether you are going to allow them to nibble away at you and your mission slowly, or whether you'll force them to take you down in one big chomp.

***

When I gave my first keynote speech that brought down the house, I knew I'd made it. The swell of impressed emails, phone calls, and clients gave me new energy to hone the presentation I'd already poured all of myself into. Soon enough, I had so much more than a great presentation—I had a surefire audience pleaser.

Like many elite performers in the public sphere, I thrive on words of affirmation. But the applause was getting less and less fulfilling. I could do this speech—and even customize it for my audience—underwater and straitjacketed like Houdini. I loved speaking, but I was getting bored.

On a whim, when a group called YPO asked me to come in and speak, I submitted a proposal for a brand-new presentation—a speech I had not even fully conceptualized, much less written or practiced. It seemed like a safe enough opportunity to practice new material: YPO stands for "Young Presidents' Organization," and I'd read up on them just enough to see that the qualifications for membership were becoming CEO of a sizeable company before the age of forty-five. Young, ambitious, elite performers have always been my bread and butter; if I was bombing, I could just lasso them with NBA insider stories and all would be forgiven.

I booked the gig, but as the date drew closer, I realized I had *no* time to really put together something new. I was on the road, speaking, coaching, and talking to publishers about my next book. My wife, my invaluable soundboard, was busy in her new role as a producer, pitching her first show concept to all the network bigwigs. With just three days remaining, I hopped on a quick Zoom call to dazzle my business partner with an impromptu performance.

And she wasn't dazzled.

I spent all but maybe ten hours of the next seventy-two plotting, organizing, and coming up with a full blueprint of the new talk. I learned how to whiteboard. I made new graphics. I constructed entirely new tools to teach, and an airtight structure for the speech. I constructed a new model to analyze a common leadership problem.

I was exhausted by the time I walked into the lobby of the Newport Beach Country Club with my hands full of workshop materials, but I was also confident. My new presentation wasn't just good—it was outstanding. It provided more value than the award-winning speech I'd gotten bored with presenting. It had even finally shone brightly enough to dazzle my undazzle-able business partner—and I was about to walk into a room filled with young, hungry, energetic leaders like myself, looking to learn and grow. They would be absolutely blown away! No doubt, I would get a standing ovation; shoot, I would probably be speaking at every YPO chapter throughout the country after this.

As I opened the door to my waiting audience, my heart sank to my toes. These "young" presidents *all* had gray hair and matching facial expressions, signaling like roadside flares that they were *not* impressed. They were absolutely not the audience I'd thought I would be speaking to, and it looked like I was not the speaker they'd been expecting, either. You could practically see the thought-bubbles above their heads: "What can this kid teach us?" "What in the world does he think he's doing with all these arts and crafts supplies?" "What kind of dog and pony show is this?"

The organizer greeted me hurriedly, and commanded me to keep engagement high: "We've given you two hours. Use them wisely. We recently cut off Nelson Mandela's attorney after thirty minutes because he wasn't engaging enough."

Yikes. I was in trouble.

All the moisture I usually keep in my throat—you know, to make the words come out—ran straight to my palms as the YPO members went around the wine dungeon, stating their names, the companies they ran, and their net worth. Not one of them cracked a smile.

As the last guy wrapped up his uber-impressive bio, the clock at the end of the long oak table started its 120-minute countdown and all eyes swiveled to me.

I stammered through the intro, missing lines I wanted to hit, unsure if I had even tied together the main points of the talk. This audience was giving me nothing—no chuckles at my jokes, not even a polite head nod. Ten agonizing minutes in with absolutely no affirmation, I wondered if I should just throw in the towel. At this point, only these eleven men would know I was a huge failure; it wouldn't crush my speaking career to quit right now. But if I bombed for the full two hours, I had no idea if I'd even be able to rally myself to climb in front of an audience ever again. The gossip would be hard to live down if they started chucking tomatoes at me.

Suddenly, a voice inside my head drowned out my audience's silence: "You're okay. You have God and you have your wife. What more do you need?"

Instantly, I felt at peace. I went on autopilot and flawlessly delivered the model. I was outside of my body, watching myself speak. I didn't feel at all like I was in control of the words coming out of my mouth, but they continued coming—and man, they were *good*.

The eleven men who'd considered me an afternoon snack slowly began to engage. It was just one chuckle or nod at a time, but by the time we hit the activities, they were cackling and high-fiving their counterparts across the table. When my 120 minutes were up, these not-at-all-young presidents begged me to stay for a few extra minutes, thanked me heartily, and offered to help me on my journey in any way possible. I'd not only made it through that talk, but I'd absolutely dominated it. I got a lot of affirmation from some of the most powerful men in Southern California. I'd impressed them, even when they'd been determined not to be impressed.

And I'd grown exponentially as a speaker, because I realized their affirmation wasn't the real win of the day, *at all*. I discovered the piece that had been missing, the reason I was so bored with my award-winning surefire speech: audience affirmation isn't validation.

I'd long been confident that I could impress high-level business leaders with a talk—but even if this room had never warmed up to me, I didn't need their validation. They never even had a chance to eat me alive. I didn't need anything from them. I had God and my wife and a genuinely amazing concept, even if no one else in the room recognized it. This breakthrough confidence gave me grace. I didn't have to perform, or worry about impressing these people, or fear failure. I had breakthrough confidence in who I was, and no one in that room—or any other room—could give that to me *or* take it away.

Intimidation and fear are powerful teachers, and I think every elite performer owes a lot to them. We don't even necessarily need to be rejected—just needing the validation, even if we're getting it all the time, can wreck breakthrough confidence. One of my closest friends is Jeremy Lin. I didn't know Jeremy at the height of the Lin-Sanity phenomenon, during the 2011–2012 season when he led the New York Knicks to a turnaround winning season, but I certainly knew about it—we all did! He was the number one trending news story around the globe. As thankful and grateful as Jeremy was for it all, he would *never* want to go through it again. He wrestled with constant what ifs: What if I stop performing at this level? What if I can't keep this up? What will people think of me? With the lights and cameras always on him, he wasn't able to enjoy the moment; he was always worried about what was coming next.

And that is a problem universal to high performers! Those what-ifs are the natural result when elite performers focus on "hows"—a stumbling block that keeps us stuck searching for just a singular breakthrough, completely barring entry to the breakthrough lifestyle. As much as you've done, built, and accomplished, the world's expectations can play games with your mind. Most of us will never experience it at the level Jeremy did, but we can all relate to how burdensome those expectations can be. Watching Jeremy come into his own as a person—standing up for his Taiwanese people, his faith, and his gourmet cooking skills—and helping him on the path to finding true breakthrough confidence has been one of the greatest honors of my career.

You've been thrown around like a rag doll at some point, chewed up and spit out when you walked into a situation filled with more incompetent ego than you could back up with talent, strength, and results. You built up your powers after recognizing that the judgment of others could leave you paralyzed with fear, choking on your words, completely unable to bring your full potential to the table. You are shaped more by the scorn of your detractors than by your standing ovations. You've obsessed over developing your skills to the highest levels so you can never be intimidated like that again.

But that externally based confidence can only carry you through so much. You might make the best sales pitch in the world, an offer no one could possibly refuse—but if your confidence is reliant on someone else's "yes," any "no" will eat you alive. There will always be new rooms, filled with bigger, more intimidating bosses who have no problem giving you that bone crushing "no." Breakthrough confidence is being grateful for these opportunities to hone your skills and take stock of who you are at your core and what truly validates you. It's being intimidated *not* to enter these rooms—to *not* hold your ideas up to the hottest fires.

Whose validation do you need—and whose rejection can eat you alive?

***

The greatest fear we have isn't of being rejected. It's not the fear of death. It's not even the fear of showing up naked for a public talk.

Our greatest fear is the fear of the unknown.

The longer we go without a breakthrough, the bigger the worst-case scenarios in our heads grow. We might remain confident in our abilities, but we aren't confident at all that we can keep the worst case from playing out before our eyes—despite the fact that most of our worst-case scenarios never actually happen. Falling vending machines kill more people each year than sharks, but you don't shudder in fear each time you grab a

Snickers from your office death threat. It is known. It is rarely actively toppling over, in your experience. But when you're suspended underwater in a cage surrounded by sharks, it doesn't matter how confident you are in your scuba skills—the idea that you're about to get eaten is going to take a top spot in your thoughts.

In 2013, I was playing professional basketball in Adelaide, Australia (which more closely resembled Will Ferrell's *Semi-Pro* than any NBA game you've seen). We had the weekend off from games, and a teammate told me I was one short plane ride away from shark diving in Port Lincoln. As a self-proclaimed adrenaline junkie (despite a deathly fear of heights over four stories), I wasn't about to pass up this adventure!

I woke up at the crack of dawn, grabbed a terrible coffee, and skipped with excitement down the pier to the boat that would take me in search of the most deadly, fear-provoking beast of the sea: the great white shark. My goal was simple: I would stare down the monsters, and they would blink first. (Yeah, I know sharks don't blink. But they would today. They would have to—I would blind them with my confidence.)

When the captain finally dropped the anchor three hours into the choppy journey, I was more afraid of continued sea sickness than any prehistoric beast.

"Who's ready to hop in?" the captain asked in his very thick Australian accent.

My hand shot up. I'd like to claim this was bravery, but I would have done anything to get off this boat for even a second.

As I hopped into the wetsuit and strapped on my mask and oxygen tank, the captain threw out a massive tuna, chummed and bleeding, to attract the savage sharks. At first, I was fascinated by the size of the tuna—I couldn't remember ever seeing a whole one, and I guess the size of the StarKist cans had led me to believe they were much, much smaller. The size of the tuna was quickly put into stark perspective as it attracted a swarm of sharks, each of whom was at least ten feet long.

I climbed into the cage and hit the water, sinking between the sharks and into two diametrically opposed feelings. I was intensely afraid—and completely calm. The water was cloudy and peaceful; I couldn't see any movement. But I knew the sharks were out there, complete with razor-sharp teeth, and I knew that at some point, they would take an interest in me.

Sitting in the corner of a cage deep in the Pacific Ocean, at a location no one would have been able to access if Jaws had decided he *really* wanted me for a mid-morning snack, I realized I had it all wrong. I wasn't afraid of the mysterious, dangerous, unknown sharks. They weren't really unknown—I knew for a fact that the waters were infested with great whites. I'd just seen them tear through tuna after tuna.

No, the unknown was *when* they were going to strike, *when* they would rattle the cage, *when* they'd break through and attempt to bite my head off in one chomp. The real fear was in the timing. It's *always* in the timing.

As elite performers, we want to be in control; we want our destinies determined by our actions. Our worst-case scenarios may or may not come true, but terrible, sad things we can do *nothing* to change will absolutely happen. Our loved ones will die; that's known. Our bodies and our brains will not always work at the levels they do now; everything comes to an end. We just don't know when.

Breakthrough confidence doesn't give you the ability to see the future, control time and space, or even develop elite skills strong enough to take down a swarm of sharks. It's not going to make any great fearsome beast blink. It's recognizing that ultimately, you have no control over the greatest unknowns. None at all. There is no answer to the question "Who are you?" that can provide that control—and breakthrough confidence is recognizing that searching for that mastery is an impassable roadblock to answering your "how." Breakthrough confidence appreciates the peace of the plunge. We never know when our underwater cage will turn into a horror show, but if we insist on timing the ending, we will miss the beautiful moments, the remarkable feelings, and the joyful rhythm of life. Breakthrough confidence isn't about eliminating all the fear factors; it's about not allowing them to control who you are and where your breakthrough is heading right now. Let the sharks eat you alive when they decide it's time to eat you alive—just don't let anticipation and worry eat you alive every second of every day before that.

Your breakthrough needs to happen before the massive shareholders meeting? Shareholders are going to be shareholders. If they want to eat you alive, they will, even if you kill yourself trying to make them happy. When you stop basing your confidence on trying to control the numbers to please the shareholders, you will have a breakthrough that generates even better results. You can replace "shareholders" with "family," "team," or any other group you're trying to control the unknown for. Breakthrough confidence is driving towards your expansion and inviting others to expand with you. You lose it when you dictate (much less let anyone else dictate!) the terms of what your expansion will look like every quarter, even if you're supremely confident you'll hit the target. Someday, something in that murky water will absolutely eat you alive. Breakthrough confidence is refusing to live like you can set that date.

I didn't get eaten by a great white that day. I didn't conquer fear or time, or develop confidence in my ability to fight off a shark. I developed breakthrough confidence that I had zero control over the sharks. I accepted the past. I appreciated the present. I could fully anticipate the future. I grew because I finally knew, without a doubt, that someday, something was going to eat me alive. I wasn't going to spend another ounce of energy on trying to control it. I was going to pour it all into the breakthroughs I could have in between.

Who are you trying to control the unknown for?

WHOSE OPPORTUNITY IS THIS?

Who the heck questions a great opportunity? Not you! You are driven. You create your own opportunities, you press for more, and you never let one pass you by. You have the confidence to seize any opportunity and drive it like you stole it.

Full disclosure? I've never stolen a car. Not even close. But I am familiar with the lingo. (I know a person or two who may have in their day.) Hot-wiring a car is "boosting." It rarely turns out well.

Not every potential opportunity is for you. And that's okay! Don't steal someone else's breakthrough opportunity just because you are trying to boost yourself. Your opportunity will come, just not in the package of a hot-wired 1964 Pontiac GTO.

Living with breakthrough confidence involves critically examining every opportunity. It's as much about identifying the strengths you *don't* have as the ones you do. It's about embracing them for what they are and figuring out what they are not. Not so you can develop every skill, but so that you can identify the opportunities that are actually *your* opportunities.

Do you have the breakthrough confidence to question amazing opportunities that come your way?

***

In the spring of 2019, I was committed to becoming a best-selling author, filling arenas worldwide, speaking motivation and encouragement to thousands upon thousands. I was marrying the woman of my dreams in just a few short days. We had our home picked out. Life was nothing but forward momentum.

And then the Phoenix Suns approached me to take over their development program and give it a much-needed facelift—like what I'd done for the Brooklyn Nets, but on an even larger scale. They were prepared to give me everything I was asking for—full autonomy, movement specialists, nutritionists, sports science experts, you name it. I could build something the NBA had never seen before—a full scale "training of the future" protocol. A once-in-a-lifetime opportunity.

The night of the NBA draft lottery, I sat out on my rooftop, scanning the horizon over the water in Marina del Rey, saying goodbye to my home in California and preparing to sign my Suns contract the next day.

Suddenly, a text popped up from Jon Gordon: "David, congratulations on Phx. That will be a fun opportunity. Remember though, the enemy of great is not bad. . . ."

For some reason, my mind wandered back to a strange day on the UCLA courts. I'd been working out two players when a rush of people came in to block off the other side of the gym.

I was burning with curiosity, but after a few minutes of trying to peek around and see what basketball royalty was hidden behind the curtain, I came to terms with the fact I might never know. Security was beyond tight—my court was on lockdown.

I was just about to leave when someone rushed out to flag me down: "Hey, is this your court?"

I smiled, unsure of how to answer. Was he asking if I owned UCLA? No, I did not. Was he asking if I'd booked the courts for this time? Well, yes, I had, but I certainly wasn't going to muscle out Kobe or LeBron or whoever merited this kind of clout.

I guess he read my pause as a yes, because, with all the intensity of a doctor on a medical drama, he said, "We're down a player. We're going to need you to come in and fill the spot."

My heart beat faster in my chest as I was rushed through the curtain and came face to face with . . . Kanye West.

I don't care if you love him or hate him as a musician, a producer, or a human being, you have to acknowledge that Kanye West is one of the most important and influential artistic figures of our age. Whatever he touches, from records to fashion to news cycles, he dominates.

So, imagine my surprise when I realized that Kanye was just an okay basketball player.

What was more shocking? *He was okay with being just okay.* He was standing on court with one of the top shooting coaches in the world, but he wasn't pressing me for tips or trying to optimize his potential. He wasn't seizing the opportunity to improve. He was having fun playing with his friends, and he was fine with the fact that I was better than them.

He knew he was not on his court.

Yes, Kanye West taught me a lesson in graceful humility.

I'm forever grateful to both Kanye and Jon for the reminder. That text hit me where it mattered, and just in the nick of time. I knew where my heart was, what my goals and dreams were. It was so close, I could almost taste it—but when a new opportunity floated right in front of me, I almost took it. I'd lost sight of my breakthrough confidence to create and seize *my* opportunities. That opportunity with the Phoenix Suns was incredible, but it wasn't *mine*. Basketball got me on courts with NBA superstars, business tycoons, and even Kanye, but it wasn't where I wanted to play forever. My passion had pivoted. I had to fully understand that it's okay to walk away from the things that are no longer serving you.

Don't turn down every opportunity that isn't a direct shot straight to your breakthrough; you'll need to seize many opportunities to take you to the top of your mountain. But don't compromise and distort your breakthrough by walking down a completely different path. The enemy of great is not bad. The enemy of great is good.

Whose opportunities are you seizing?

***

When I met Amin, he was the human equivalent of an old-school pressure cooker. Just looking at him, you knew either the job was going to get done—or he was going to explode. He'd started as a video intern with the Phoenix Suns already laser-focused on his aspirations of becoming an NBA GM.

Working your way to the top in the NBA is often celebrated, but very, very rarely actually happens. The dream attracts the fiercest competition, the hardest workers, and the biggest schemers. Out of all of them, if I'd needed to bet on anyone to pull out the win through sheer willpower, it would have been Amin. He put everything he had into it—and then some. He had the hunger to be influential, to be recognized for his talents and observations. This dude *pressed*.

And then . . . everyone on staff was let go. Amin was back at the beginning. All that time, effort, energy, momentum—gone.

He didn't even finish brushing himself off before he started searching for the next job, the next team, the next opportunity to start working his way up once again. The only "break" he took from his singular focus was more of a favor to a friend, who'd asked him to write a sample piece for ESPN.com.

That throwaway article was so well received that Amin was offered a ten-article freelance gig; those ten articles were so well received that, in 2013, ESPN hired him on full time. He quickly shot up the ranks to become one of the most loved, hated, and undeniably magnetic voices at the most important sports network in the world.

Today, Amin Elhassan is one of the most well-known faces on sports television. When we go out for lunch he wears hats and sunglasses and uses a comic-book-type alias to stay under the radar—a far cry from the video intern who was always on a full-court press. He's made it to the top of a field with stiffer competition than any NBA GM position, at a company that thousands of people study for years just to get the chance to intern with. In Amin's own words, "If you look at the media landscape, almost all the analysts who have come from the league side are former players or other very big-name people. Rarely, if ever, do you see the nuts-and-bolts worker bees that populate most NBA front offices."

Amin has made it—not as a GM, but as someone even more influential and recognized in the NBA. He paused his press to embrace the opportunity that was actually his. Did it look like the great opportunities that he was chasing with reckless confidence? Not at all. But those great opportunities weren't the greatest opportunities for him. He earned his breakthrough with the breakthrough confidence to seize a less obviously glamorous opportunity that fit him perfectly.

Pressing. Every high-achiever does it, and it drives you nuts. Yeah, determination gets you farther than most people ever dare to dream—but pressing never gets you that full 100 percent.

I was determined to be great every time I stepped on the basketball court. I wanted it so bad, I would do anything to make it happen. But when something went off course (which happens in every game—just like any other aspect of life), I'd get flustered and press harder and harder, just to watch the "great" game slip away.

Think about it—the love interest you tried to woo by being at their beck and call. The boss for whom you completely restructured your workflow. The audience you tried to impress by radically changing your style. The toy you needed to have. The battle you had to win. Even when you emerge victorious, there's something hollow in the triumph, right? These are Pyrrhic victories—when you've sacrificed so much to win that you ultimately still lose.

When you press, you've inevitably lost sight of what you actually need. You've tunneled in too far on a highly specific result. With those blinders on, everything short of that result is failure. You can no longer see the opportunities to make a difference in your field—you're too pressed on getting that job. You can no longer see the opportunities for healthy, loving relationships—you're too pressed on that person. You cannot divorce yourself from the fear of failing; you're blind to better, different opportunities. When you've thrown all your determination and strength towards opportunities that just won't budge, you still inevitably create movement in the area. If you just turn your head slightly, an even more incredible opportunity is likely staring you straight in the face.

Stop driving towards opportunities that aren't yours. Don't compromise your breakthrough confidence by pressing against opportunities that the world might see as better. If you're in a tug of war with a great opportunity that just won't budge, have the breakthrough confidence to drop it. You need your hands free to seize the opportunities that are actually yours for the taking.

Whose opportunities are you pressing on?

***

Understanding that not every great opportunity is *your* opportunity leads to some obvious questions: *Whose is it?! Am I supposed to just leave great opportunities on the ground? What if MY opportunity isn't coming?*

The best way to guarantee that you'll never find *your* opportunity is continually seizing, driving, and pressing on the wrong ones. Breakthrough confidence is moving through daily life with the peace and comfort of knowing that you're creating the opportunities you need by refusing the ones you don't. When you drive people nuts with your full court press, they won't want to work in breakthrough cooperation with you when they have the next opportunity—the one that might be *exactly* what you need. When you take opportunities that aren't yours, you're not available when your own opportunity arises.

Should you just leave great opportunities on the ground— heck no! BIOnic leaders are *always* leveraging their experience, knowledge, and opportunities to grow the people around them. That great opportunity that isn't yours? You promote and champion the person you know it would be amazing for. You work in breakthrough cooperation with the talented, skilled, elite performers you surround yourself with. How valuable was it—or how valuable would it have been—for you to work alongside BIOnic leaders to get where you are today? The great opportunities that aren't yours are still great opportunities for you—to give back and expand your influence in service to others.

No single elite performer has all the strengths needed to break through. The more breakthrough confident you are, the more excited you become to cataloging all your skills and strengths—and *especially* your weaknesses. Recognizing your weaknesses isn't shameful—it's awesome. That's the complements wish list that guides your breakthrough cooperation. Let's shift to Q2 and meet your team!

BREAKTHROUGH CONFIDENCE KEYS

- Specialize in your elite strength.

- Examine your flaws for hidden gifts.

- Embrace imposter syndrome.

- The greatest control is knowing you're not in control.

- Stop pressing.

- Recognize your opportunities.

BREAKTHROUGH CONFIDENCE TOOL: HEAR IT FROM THE SOURCE

Want results 100 times faster than what you're seeing? Use your ears!

We hear faster than we see, so jumpstart your breakthrough confidence at the beginning of your breakthrough day, and start Q1 of your morning by verbalizing and creating an audio recording of your progress. This activity is part gratitude journaling, part pump-up note, and 100 percent appreciation for who you are.

Approach this with a full commitment to total honesty *and* positivity. Don't massage a moment in the past when you defaulted to operating in confidence rather than breakthrough confidence, and don't berate yourself. You accept your past. Don't get sarcastic or judgmental about the day ahead. You anticipate your breakthrough future. This is all for your ears only.

Equipment Required: Recording Device (Notes app on your phone or computer), Script

Space Required: Private, No Distractions

Time Required: <2 Minutes

Instructions:

1. Listen to yesterday's "Let's Hear It for Our Hero!" file. (Obviously, you're going to skip step 1 on your first day!)

2. Take one full minute to read the script below and reflect on how you're going to fill in the blanks for today's message.

3. Start recording and make it happen!

4. Label and save the file some place private that you can easily access tomorrow.

Script:

Hey (<u>my name or nickname</u>)!

Thanks for reacting to (<u>insert a difficult situation from yesterday</u>) so well. I'm really grateful for the breakthrough confidence to acknowledge fear and uncertainty without losing sight of my mission.

Instead of settling for mediocrity and going through the motions yesterday, I focused on my strengths when (<u>insert an incident from yesterday when I chose to operate in my elite strength</u>). Accepting (<u>insert an attribute I previously considered a flaw</u>) has significantly improved my breakthrough confidence and the amount of energy I have to dedicate to my breakthrough.

I'm so excited to continue developing my breakthrough confidence today by reaching for (<u>insert something outside my comfort zone</u>). Whatever the result, it's going to be a huge win in my breakthrough process!

Thanks for being the breakthrough yesterday, today, and tomorrow. We're amazing!

CHAPTER 3

Q2: Smelling What: Breakthrough Cooperation

As you move into the second quarter of your day, shift your focus to the "what"—what relationships matter?

Your daily breakthrough success isn't tied to what you got on your SATs, the prestige of the college you attended, what you do for a job, how big your house is, or even how elite your strengths are—it's all about your relationships. You don't focus on breakthrough confidence first because *you* come first—you work on your breakthrough confidence first so you're giving your absolute best to your team.

Routinely scheduling and creating breakthroughs requires relying on others. And not just for the little stuff or side jobs: you need to truly partner with people and trust them to play intricate roles. You cannot and will not achieve any significant breakthrough without cooperation. All the people who have changed the world—every mad scientist and inventor, tech innovator, artist, religious figure, writer, and doctor you can name—worked intensely in breakthrough cooperation with others.

Trusting in external variables? Not making it all happen yourself? Those are very tough pills for elite performers swallow. Trust me, I know! I was laser-focused on playing in the NBA for twenty years, and I didn't have the type of talent that attracts an entourage at a young age. The grind-it-out path is hard and lonely, but I took pride in the idea that one day, I'd be a self-made man.

I fought my way through the international basketball circuit like a man possessed, and it drove me crazy that not all my teammates were as committed and motivated. In Athens, I practiced to the point of collapse every day, while my Aussie teammate, Aron Baynes, played like he was half asleep and kicked my butt every time.

Do you think I wanted to share credit for my hard-fought success with *anyone*, much less some loafer who just happened to ooze talent from every inch of his seven-foot frame? Definitely not.

On our very last day as teammates, I finally broke and asked Aron why he even bothered playing a game he so obviously disliked. He was shocked—he was actually obsessed with basketball, and had no idea anyone thought otherwise. We spent the last few hours before flying home digging into motivations and perceptions and perspectives deeply. I ended up giving this guy—my basketball nemesis—some advice and mindset coaching to help him get to the next level.

When we finished, Aron gave me a hug and said, "Thank you for being a friend and caring about me, mate. It means a lot."

And you know what? It meant a lot to me, too. Because, for the first time since we'd met, I'd stopped focusing on everything he had and I so desperately wanted—his height, his talent. I'd stopped competing against his strengths and used my own *actual* skills to complement his. In the taxi to the airport, I realized that I had finally joined the team.

And a few months later, when I turned on the San Antonio Spurs game and saw Aron Baynes in his number 17 jersey, playing with the joy I'd coached him on, I realized that my strengths could make the NBA better in a way I'd never considered. I could be a critical component of other people's breakthroughs. *I wasn't a player—I was a coach.* It was a world-altering breakthrough for me, and Aron shares credit for that.

Whether you acknowledge it or not, you've relied on and benefited from breakthrough cooperation every day of your life.

We romanticize the mythical lone genius for many reasons, and all of them stink. Which is ironic, because the eighteenth-century scientists and philosophers who really pushed the idea that breakthroughs are solo endeavors are the same people who demoted the sense of smell. In a rush to make the world more clinical and rational, we stopped relying on our primal instincts. We disconnected from building our tribes in favor of building ourselves (how many of your connections on LinkedIn are you actually emotionally invested in?). This is probably going to sound a little weird, but building the best team requires not just your eyes and ears, but also your nose. We all have an innate ability to "sniff out" people who will lead us to our breakthroughs, and the rotten apple people who are less than genuine. Don't worry—we'll unpack the answers together. Trust me, I've got a nose for this type of thing.

I designed my very first mindset tool shortly after I realized I wanted to become an NBA shooting coach. I couldn't just call myself a coach—I had to become one. Someone had to hire me.

I knew most hires were made through network connections, and I had a great network—for *playing* basketball. I didn't have any connections with the NBA GMs and coaches who hired shooting specialists. So I started from scratch and networked like crazy, cold calling and showing up at games and offices, doing whatever I could to make myself known. Networking isn't exactly novel (although few throw themselves into it with the intensity I did), but as I started to make headway, I built out my Golden 15: fifteen connections in my industry who particularly inspired and challenged me. I knew these GMs, coaches, and team owners were frequently approached by people who wanted something from them. That was not going to be me. I decided I would help them in any way possible, and I made a special effort to genuinely connect with them. I built up equity and friendship through giving, giving, and giving without ever expecting anything in return. Just their presence in my life helped me grow, although when they realized I had no ulterior motives, they often became exceedingly generous mentors, advisors, and champions.

The Golden 15 was so effective that I still use it, and it's one of the most popular tools I teach. Learning to connect in meaningful ways isn't the difference between a big breakthrough and a small one—it's the difference between having a good idea and bringing it to life.

The Golden 15 is great, but it was really designed to connect with mentors and experts. Some members of your breakthrough team will be mentors, but there are many other roles to fill too, so there will be many more questions to ask yourself: Whom do you need on your core team? Whom do you rely on each day? What are they capable of? What can you offer them in support? This is a critical moment in your breakthrough day. You are creating more hands to do the breakthrough work, empowering people to join you on a mission, and addressing the talents you're not bringing to the breakthrough.

By really examining the full scope of your strengths with breakthrough confidence, you can also see what's missing. I don't care who you are; you don't have 'em all. Not possible. You wouldn't want 'em all even if it *was* possible! Even the most competitive elite performer has to admit that if they really want to be fluent in all 852 of the living languages of Papua New Guinea, they might only be mediocre at preparing some of the 31 different Indian cuisines while they speed-read the 4 million books published in the U.S. last year.

Instead of trying to develop all our weaknesses into strengths, we make judgments about which ones are important. Even if you work hard to keep that type of thinking contained to yourself and developing your skills, it tends to leak out in judgment of others or in your perception of how the world works. It can absolutely ruin breakthrough cooperation.

I'm not a naturally judgmental person *and* I make conscious efforts not to judge others *and* I work the breakthrough formula every day—*and* I still found myself caught up in this type of thinking not too long ago. My wife is in show business, so big Hollywood events are a part of the job; I, of course, am her designated arm candy. (Or so I like to think.) A name kept popping up, someone all the actors were working with: Jim Kwik. Jim is a learning expert and an elite memorization coach who's worked with Elon Musk, Will Smith, the *X-Men* cast, and so many others. After hearing so much about him at these big events, I was thrilled to have dinner with him—think about the stories this guy must have!

That dinner wasn't anything like the deep-dish session I was expecting. I'm a talker—I can easily hold a lively conversation for hours with a stuffed animal—but Jim wasn't from the same mold. I was shocked to find out he was a true introvert. One-on-one, he keeps his cards close.

Months later, when a friend asked me to go hear Jim give a talk, I nearly said no. I knew Jim was brilliant, but after our dinner, I figured there was just no way he'd be powerful on stage. *Speakers have to love speaking*—right?

Nope. I have never seen someone dominate a stage like Jim does. He is *captivating*. When he's presenting, he's fully engaged with his passion.

I left that talk bubbling over with excitement and with the knowledge that I still had some breakthrough confidence work to do. My internalized judgments of what strengths are critical for public speaking were way off—and that's my field! I nearly missed an amazing speech and a breakthrough lesson. Jim and I walk onto the same stages, but with completely different elite strengths; it is inspirational and a genuine breakthrough to learn new modes of playing the game and moves I never would have considered. I'm so grateful to Jim for sharing his passion with the world, and I'm committed to finding how my elite strengths can assist him—because that's someone I definitely want to be in breakthrough cooperation with for the long haul!

With breakthrough confidence in our own strengths, we better understand how they complement other people's and vice versa. The world calls our missing talents "weaknesses"—but people with breakthrough confidence recognize them as a "complements wish list." We're supposed to have different strengths to complement each other. We're supposed to work together.

Being the best alone is absolutely impossible. Determine what team members you need to operate at full capacity and what additional skills and talents you need in order to execute your breakthrough solutions. Q2 determines whether your breakthrough day is a rich perfume or a total stink bomb—you're the mix master!

WHAT ARE YOUR HEROES DOING?

You're elite, you're well networked, you're driven. Who are the first people you want to recruit to your breakthrough team? Whom do you admire and prize the most? Your heroes, of course!

That's always been my first instinct when I'm looking for breakthrough cooperation. My heroes have achieved something I want—why wouldn't I ask for directions from people who've already been to the breakthrough I want? Original inventions are rare—most breakthroughs are innovations, remixing things and ideas that already exist. Someone has taken the path you're embarking on and successfully done what you want to do. That's great for you! Compare yourself to the greatest ones in your field, emulate what they do, study who they are. Pay attention to how they play the game, and try to glean what has made them so successful and which of their breakthrough detours you want to avoid. Try to get in the room with them. Take the chance to approach them when the opportunity arises.

But don't get so starstruck that you forget your mission.

Recruiting your heroes to your breakthrough team requires taking off any rose colored glasses you may be wearing and seeing them for who they truly are. As a BIOnic leader, you have to put the breakthrough first. Breakthrough cooperation is about getting a good sense of who someone truly is and figuring out whether you admire them, want to emulate them, or truly need them on your breakthrough team.

***

My mind was set: I would coach in the NBA. Now all I needed to figure out was how the heck to get in. Everyone promised they would outwork the competition; I did a *very* little bit of math, and realized that we couldn't all outwork each other. I needed to craft my own way in, to find a door everyone wasn't pushing past each other to run in. Rather than relying on the sheer power of perspiration or hard work to get noticed, I'd develop my own God-given ability to shoot a basketball and become the best shooting coach in the NBA.

San Antonio Spurs' Chip Engelland was the gold standard of NBA shooting coaches. He was the million-dollar-per-year man who took athletes like Tony Parker, Tim Duncan, and Kawhi Leonard—players who couldn't hit the broad side of a barn when they first came into the league—and turned them into top shooters. If I could emulate his every move and develop myself in his image, I'd be made.

I began to study Chip. Like, really study Chip. I watched every YouTube video I could find on him teaching players how to shoot, I read every article, I even tuned in to every Spurs game just to see how he interacted with the players and the other coaches during the game.

But all this watching and reading just wasn't making the cut. It felt mechanical and sterile. Down at the park, mimicking

Chip's moves step by step, I felt more like a robot than the beast I needed to be to make the NBA.

I was distracted by two dogs passing each other on the nearby sidewalk. I watched in amazement as they went from semi-hostile strangers on opposing leashes to BFFs in less than a minute. They sniffed each other out and knew instantly that they were on the same team. That was *exactly* what I needed! Watching all the game film in the world wasn't going to cut it—I needed to get a sense of who Chip was. If we could just sniff each other out, I knew we'd be on the same team.

I found his phone number, sucked up every ounce of pride, and made the call.

Crickets.

Email? Same deal. Handwritten letter? No response.

Luckily, I had another in—my buddy and former teammate Aron Baynes was playing for Chip in San Antonio. Aron could certainly convince Chip to give me a chance—just ten minutes was all I needed.

I texted Aron, and he got back to me the same day: "Sorry, mate, Chip said he wasn't interested."

So I did what any totally sane person would do: I drove to Las Vegas and posted up outside the Summer League gym, hoping to catch him.

Three days later, Chip started the long walk down the corridor of the Thomas & Mack Center towards me, carrying a black notebook I was convinced held all the earthly secrets to shooting. I held my breath and caught his eyes just as he caught mine. The moment of semi-hostile lock-in and split-second judgment we all make (consciously or subconsciously) was on. For the first time, I wondered if I really was a big dog. Only one way to tell—I had to strain my leash.

"Chip!" I said, walking straight to him with a big smile on my face and my hand extended.

I could tell he didn't know who I was—and there was no reason for him to. But whatever big dog instinct I'd been relying on played out real-time, right in front of my eyes. He grinned like he was meeting a cousin for the first time in years. Chip greeted me with a warm handshake and a very firm pat on the back: "Walk with me, kid."

On our way into the arena, Chip peppered me with questions—not easy ones, no surface-level fluff. I must have passed the test, and I got a real sense of who Chip was—maybe even more from the energy he asked the questions with than their content alone.

Throughout the game, Chip shared everything he had done to get to where he was and how I could do the same. He gave me tips I'd never heard before and haven't heard from anyone else since, like "Use your sister as your business manager when you deal with money from NBA players, you'll look more professional," "Never make the workout about you, always make it about what you can give the player," and "Don't take pictures with players unless they give you permission—you want to be friends with them when you are eighty years old, not just use and burn." The advice was invaluable, this one afternoon completely shaped the way I coach players, approach the business of being a shooting coach, and just the way I treat others, putting their needs and comfort before my own.

To this day, I couldn't even tell you what teams were playing in that game, nor did I care. Chip laid out a blueprint to achieve my dreams. I owe him a lot. He gave me exactly what I needed, and none of that could have happened if I hadn't been able to seek out Chip and figure out how we were alike, how we were different, and what I wanted to emulate from his excellent example and experience.

Figure out who you want to be *like*, not who you want to *be*. Breakthroughs become much easier when we recognize that there is someone who has done something similar to what we are dreaming of, or they are farther along the path than we are. There's no such thing as a 100 percent original—everything is a variation on some theme. Compare yourself to the greatest ones in your field, emulate what they do, study who they are, and create your own mixture of what is authentically you. The best aura you can ever exude: integrity with a heavy splash of authenticity. I set out to get Chip to like me, but what he gave me, the experience of knowing him, was so much more valuable.

It was definitely a breakthrough—but was it breakthrough cooperation?

I've been blessed to meet many of my heroes, and the number who have been helpful and gracious blows me away. Like Chip Engelland, Carlos Reynaldo, Jerry West, and John Mark Comer have all sat with me and imparted wisdom and guidance that I treasure and carry with me into every breakthrough. But as valuable as these one-time meetings were, I don't think we can call them true breakthrough cooperation. They were on their own breakthrough path, and mine intersected with it for a moment. I haven't been able to contribute my elite strengths to their breakthroughs yet, and I wouldn't expect them to commit any further to mine.

Other heroes who have become mentors and members of my Golden 15 include Casey Wasserman, Erik Spoelstra, and Jim Kwik. I am dedicated to helping them in any way I can, without worrying whether I ever see anything tangible in return. It's not about what I can get from them, but instead what I can provide for them. These relationships are incredibly important to me, and absolutely inform and help shape my breakthroughs.

There is a third category of heroes with whom I'm now working in breakthrough cooperation with. I know Jon Gordon, Ed Mylett, and Cori Close are invested in my breakthrough, as I am in theirs. They bring their considerable elite strengths to help me, and I am able to use mine to help them in return. It's not always an even give-and-take, but when you're on a team that lives out breakthrough cooperation, the members never keep score.

As you approach your heroes with breakthrough cooperation in mind, remember each of these three categories. They all offer unique value. Deeply appreciate the heroes who meet with you once and impart amazing wisdom and heroes that become mentors and members of your Golden 15. The dream is to work with your heroes in breakthrough cooperation, but you can't force that and you wouldn't want to. You cannot be in breakthrough cooperation with everyone—it requires mutual support.

What can you offer in support of your most generous breakthrough heroes?

***

Even as a die-hard ten-year-old Utah Jazz fan, I idolized one man and one man only on the Chicago Bulls in their most legendary years. It wasn't Michael Jordan—it was Phil Jackson, the Zen-like coach in his mid-fifties with the long gray beard. I was mesmerized with how Coach Jackson could masterfully orchestrate the triangle offense and flow together such disparate personalities. I had no idea how he did it, much less with such a calm, peaceful disposition that he could lower even my ten-year-old ADD blood pressure. I wasn't going to cheer for him when the Bulls played my beloved Jazz, but I respected the heck out of Phil Jackson.

That admiration only increased with age, as Phil Jackson went on to coach the Los Angeles Lakers and maestro two of the biggest personalities in all of sports: Shaq and Kobe. They despised each other, but Phil made this unlikely marriage of egos work—no, thrive—without breaking a sweat. Phil Jackson led the Lakers, a team of incredible talent that would have absolutely imploded without his guidance, to their first three-peat NBA Championship run. The last team that had done that? Yeah, the Chicago Bulls—under the coaching of Phil Jackson.

After my experience with Chip, I was set to become an NBA shooting coach—but I toyed with the possibility of becoming an NBA head coach, so I knew I needed to meet Phil. Who better to learn the intricacies of the game from than this living legend?

Once again, I found myself at Thomas & Mack Center in Las Vegas for NBA Summer League—the hot box living sauna that was quickly becoming my annual July home. Phil was there to watch the New York Knicks Summer League team, as he was now the president of basketball operations, hired to revitalize the always-underachieving Knicks. I was there to watch Phil for my opportunity to pounce.

My opportunity arose just as the game ended and the crowd got twenty minutes to stretch or move seats before the next tip-off. Swiftly weaving through rows, hopping over entire seats when necessary, I made my way to Phil Jackson.

I waited my turn to talk as patiently as I could, panting like an overzealous pup. Phil wrapped up his conversation, and I was practically wagging my tail.

"Yes?" Phil asked in his very deep, very Zen voice.

I spilled over about how much I admired him, how much respect I had for him, and how he was my favorite coach for as long as I could remember. I told him I aspired to be like him one day, and if I could become one-tenth the coach he was, I would be ecstatic. I waited for a response or a pat on the back, a word of encouragement to keep going, the smile that Chip had granted me. I didn't need the hours from Phil that Chip had given me—even just ten minutes would boost me for years.

Phil simply nodded his head, turned, and started a conversation with the Knicks' staff member sitting behind him.

I was crushed. I knew Phil had sensed my eagerness and determination, yet he completely blew me off. I couldn't run with him. Embarrassed and extremely let down, I walked back to my seat with my tail between my legs.

My idol, my coaching role model, didn't want anything to do with me.

I never talked to Phil again, but other coaches assured me it wasn't just me. His nickname was "Two-Minute Phil" because he didn't give anyone more than two minutes of his time. He wasn't looking for breakthrough cooperation, and after getting a two-second experience of him, I realized I didn't want his either. I will always admire, respect, and appreciate Phil Jackson's incredible coaching abilities, but I will never try to emulate or incorporate his style. I met my hero and realized our styles just didn't match.

We put our idols on extremely high pedestals. We can aspire to be like them, we can study and emulate everything they do. But this doesn't mean they are the people we want them to be. Until you rub shoulders with them, you don't really know whether you truly want to follow in their footsteps, much less be in breakthrough cooperation with them.

Of course, not all of our heroes are celebrities. Our heroes can come from anywhere—our families, jobs, and communities. Most of us would probably be more comfortable calling our parents our heroes than our boss or our neighbor, but whatever position they fill in our lives, they just exude a heroic aura.

Emotions, including happiness, fear, and disgust can often be detected, sometimes even outside of our awareness. What's crazier is that the emotions may actually be contagious. People who lose their sense of smell aren't as in tune with other's emotions, even when they're seeing the same facial expressions, and they don't "catch" the mood as easily as people who have a sense of smell. For all our other senses, our brains register the information first, then transmit our emotional reactions. Smells actually register as emotions first, so they can powerfully influence our subconscious thoughts and behavior.

In other words, when someone seems like a hero to you for no particular reason, maybe your nose knows!

Think about that person in your workplace who just seems to have it all together, who has hit their life rhythm, and who goes about their day with such a calm, peaceful pace—yet who is a top performer and accomplishes so much. How can that be? How do they have such joy and success all wrapped together in one? Stop trying to rationalize it and spend time with them. Their aura might just be infectious!

> *As a BIOnic leader, what type of energy do you want to give off, and what emotions do you want it to share with your breakthrough team?*

WHAT DO YOU VALUE MOST IN YOUR TEAM?

Okay, so some of your heroes are breakthrough cooperation material, some aren't. Either way, you're going to need a deeper bench—and more variety.

You were drawn to your heroes because you admired them and wanted to emulate them; obviously, there's going to be a lot of crossover between your elite strengths and theirs. However, your core breakthrough cooperation team has to address your complements wish list. You need cooperation from people with elite strengths you don't have, and you want to offer your elite strength in return.

Even though you may never have consciously built a breakthrough cooperation team, you've asked for guidance, accepted assistance, and even hired people to handle things you aren't qualified or equipped for. When it comes to engaging people for a task, most prefer one of two options:

1. The absolute top, best, most elite professional in the field

    or

2. Someone from their trusted close circle—as close to family as possible

Do you know which option you prefer? Before you start reading, take a guess at which one works better for breakthrough cooperation.

***

When my smart, responsible much better half graduated from college, she knew the safe move was law school. Taylor grew up just thirty miles from the center of Hollywood, so she wasn't naïve. She knew that it took a perfect alignment of talent, timing, and pure luck to make it big in the City of Lights. Most people never even line up with an agent, much less a successful audition.

But she just couldn't shake the urge to act.

When a friend's acting manager offered to represent her, Taylor was thrilled. This guy was the real deal, well established in the business with a full roster of stars. With management like this, she had a real chance to break through. Taylor knew her talent existed, but it was raw and unfinished, like a block of marble. This manager was a man who knew talent and knew potential, and had formed many fine and successful actors; he could help her chisel this block of marble into a masterpiece.

The manager set to work, chipping away at her edges, and Taylor welcomed every piece of guidance and advice. When the manager told her she was overacting, Taylor hired a personal acting coach to bolster the wide variety of acting classes she was already in. When the manager advised her that her wardrobe wasn't sophisticated enough, she dropped a pretty penny on revamping her closet. When he told her the professional modeling portfolio she'd been collecting for years didn't show the range she needed to present, she arranged headshot sessions with the photographer he recommended. When he set her up with an agent, Taylor showed up with her brightest smile and left the meeting positive that the agent really liked her. When the manager told her that he wouldn't connect them again because the agent wasn't interested in her, Taylor smiled bravely and asked for additional feedback to better prepare for the next opportunity. When he told Taylor her voice was too deep and manly, she connected with a voice coach. When the manager informed Taylor that she should get bangs because her advanced age and forehead wrinkles were an incredible hurdle, she sat in front of the mirror and genuinely tried to find these flaws.

It was true; Taylor *was* getting older. She had just reached the extremely advanced age of twenty-four, nearly two years older than when she'd started with this manager. Although she was routinely told she could play in her teens, she suddenly felt older . . . and smaller. The manager was chipping away at her, as promised, but she felt more crushed than developed. And she wasn't any closer to getting the roles she was interested in.

Taylor didn't know where to turn. She wasn't ready to quit on her dream, but she didn't want to feel this way anymore. She needed someone to talk to. She always had her parents, and they were wonderful and supportive—but she needed someone more objective, with more experience in her field.

Luckily, along the way, Taylor had developed a close professional relationship with her acting coach. When she finally opened up to him and expressed her concerns, he affirmed her growing suspicion: this manager wasn't interested in developing her. He was playing sadistic, controlling mind games.

Taylor knew she needed to get out of this toxic relationship, but it was pilot season. An actor dumping her manager before the end of pilot season is about the same as a basketball player dropping his agent the night of the NBA draft: in no way, shape, or form a good idea.

A bad team member is better than no team at all, right? That's how most of the world operates. You don't quit your job, even if it is crushing your soul, before you find something better. You don't fire your accountant, even if he can't add and subtract, before you line up a new one. You don't break up with your partner, even if the relationship has run its course, before you find a new love interest.

But Taylor had breakthrough confidence in her strengths, and she knew she needed more than just a team member—she needed breakthrough cooperation. She could look around her life and see the many people who wanted to help her grow and flourish, and whom she wanted to help in the same way. They didn't have the connections or the expertise of the manager, but he wasn't using his connections and expertise to develop her anyway. If she wanted to break through, she needed her breakthrough team. And she was finally in the position to recognize that having someone on her team who wasn't interested in cooperating on her mission was actively detrimental. The best in the business doesn't necessarily make them the best in *your* business.

Taylor took a deep breath and bet on her own breakthrough. She sent the manager an email to terminate her contract; he responded with a stream of vile verbal abuse. Taylor smiled and sent back a very kind email thanking him for his time. That's who she was, is, and always has been, and she wouldn't let the manager change anything about her ever again—not even her goodbye.

Taylor went the next four months without getting even a sniff of an audition. From the outside, it might have looked like she made the wrong call on the manager, but Taylor had breakthrough confidence and knew her mission would continue to attract members to her breakthrough team. She poured into her own development, attending five different acting classes a week when most actors can barely commit to one. She submitted herself on casting sites to raise the chances a casting director would notice her. She surrounded herself with the people she did have breakthrough cooperation with, including her friend Gabby. Even after two years with intensive management, Taylor still had zero credits to her name, so the two actresses put their heads together and created their own short film.

Now that casting directors could see how Taylor held herself on camera, they were genuinely interested. Suddenly, she was inundated with auditions—including a project she really, really wanted.

And they gave Taylor her first callback.

And then a second callback.

And then a third callback!

When you get three callbacks in Hollywood, you're in—the spot is yours.

When they called back for the fourth time, Taylor was devastated to learn that the spot was not, in fact, hers. Another actress had come in at the last moment—a big name who would help the movie secure funding. Taylor was surprised to learn that this actress was even interested in the role—until she learned the name behind the move. Yup, Taylor's own former manager was pulling the strings—still working against Taylor.

She wanted to quit. She didn't want anything to do with acting ever again—she sure as hell never wanted to set foot into another audition room. The force of her breakthrough confidence just wasn't strong enough to fight against a malicious anti-breakthrough squad.

Gabby was helping Taylor drown her sorrows in a tub of Ben & Jerry's when a new audition notification came in. A film with no title or name producers attached and little chance of being greenlit had requested Taylor's audition tape for one of the lead roles. With all the power of breakthrough cooperation one person can muster, Gabby insisted that Taylor submit. (And that truly is one of the most crucial elements of breakthrough cooperation—no one person can keep the flame alive through every twist and turn. When you have a team as committed to your mission as you are, there's someone there to hold the torch aloft when your arms are just too tired.)

Taylor submitted her audition and held her breath once more. After many days, she exhaled. No response. Taylor wrote this project off—she had the pen ready, and she was finally prepared to write off her acting career altogether. It was over before it even began; she wasn't cut out for Hollywood.

When Taylor sat at the end of her mother's bed, explaining her decision and feeling like a shell of herself, her mom put a hand on her back and said, "Taylor, this is God's way of telling you that you need to let go of control. Why don't you just take a step back and let God be God. You are going to be very busy soon; this is a time God has set aside for you to rest."

Taylor realized that in all her efforts to build breakthrough cooperation, she had been stubbornly trying to dictate the timing. If she wanted God on her breakthrough team (talk about a well-established, big-deal connection!), she had to cooperate with Him. She was in charge of developing the gifts and talents and dreams He'd given her—He was in charge of timing.

The next day, Taylor rededicated herself to developing her gifts and trusting that she would be as ready as possible when God decided the time was right. She started making an acting reel—hiring actors to put on scenes together with her to show the full range of her talent. It wasn't cheap, but Taylor walked out of that room feeling much wealthier than the $73 she had left in her account. She was pouring into her talent and developing her strength with renewed breakthrough confidence, trusting again that her mission would attract the breakthrough cooperation she needed.

Weeks later, one of the actors in Taylor's reel (and a new member of her breakthrough cooperation team) messaged her on Facebook; a friend was directing a project. Actually, it was the same project Gabby had insisted Taylor submit her audition to months before, but now it had a title: *I'm Not Ashamed*. A film about the true story of Columbine's first victim Rachel Joy Scott. The next day Taylor received a request to participate in a virtual callback session with the director.

Still, nothing went smoothly. Taylor arranged to read once again, but as she signed into the Skype audition, the power went out in all of Marina del Rey. Talk about timing. She learned on Facebook that the table read had begun before she'd even heard back about her audition. The independent film was on a tight budget, and decided to cast actors local to Nashville. All signs pointed towards no—including the hard no Taylor got from the casting director.

But these hurdles, which would have made any actor write off a project, didn't crush Taylor any longer. She had unshakable breakthrough confidence in who she was, and she was acting in breakthrough cooperation with an amazing team. She kept being true to herself—sending a kind email to the casting director's rejection and praying for the success of the project. And she trusted God with the timing. If this was the right project for her, He'd find a way.

One night, Taylor had an extremely vivid dream of an email outlining her participation in the film: flight info, set meals, everything. Hiking with Gabby the next morning, Taylor admitted she still had a burning feeling she was going to be part of this movie.

Now, Gabby is kind, considerate, and a wonderful break-through team member—but part of being truly breakthrough cooperative is refusing to be a yes-man. Taylor was fully expecting her practical friend to give her a reality check based on her own Hollywood experience and to encourage her to stop chasing a project that had already gone by.

To Taylor's surprise, Gabby nodded thoughtfully and admitted that, even though it made no sense, she was also still certain that Taylor was called to be in this film.

By the time they arrived home, the dream email was waiting. Taylor had been offered the role of Rachel Joy Scott's best friend. And they'd just renamed the character—Gabby!

Taylor flew out the next day and filmed *I'm Not Ashamed*. Not only was the project miraculously fully funded, but it was widely released all over the world and grossed millions. Taylor's breakthrough team grew as her performance caught the eye of multiple agents, managers, and publicists. The role opened doors for her career in television. And Masey McLain, the actress who played Rachel Joy Scott, became one of Taylor's best friends; they have now begun writing, pitching, and producing several shows on the biggest networks and online platforms together.

The other projects Taylor had wanted so badly, the *big* projects she'd tried to force the timing on, that her evil ex-manager had blocked her from? None of them saw the light of day. Had Taylor booked them, she would never have been free for the breakthrough she was *actually* meant for.

As high performers, we can try to beat down every door to the breakthrough on our own. We can try to make a team work without breakthrough cooperation. But until we put together the team of the best scents that work for us and our breakthrough, all we can do is hope to get there by accident.

Disconnect with the mindset that there is a "best of the best" you have to work with. Results and résumés don't speak to the values you need the people on your team to share with you. Decide the values that matter most to you and build your team from that foundation. Someone who believes in you and has the same values is always going to be a stronger long-term teammate than someone who has a shiny title. Focus on the true relational, not the facade transactional.

What values are most important to you and your breakthrough, and what would you be compromising by ignoring those values?

***

I was a junior in high school in 2003 when *Kiplinger's Personal Finance* magazine started arriving on our doorstep in Kearney, Missouri. I took it like an omen of my true calling. I just knew I was going to get rich trading stock; specifically, my detailed plan was to hit a home run right away by choosing the high-growth stock no one else knew about. Foolproof.

I transferred all the personal wealth I had amassed ($300, give or take) to E*TRADE, a mobile stock exchange website. My dad reminded me that my car would not run on future earnings alone, so after a detour to referee a middle school basketball game, I finally sat down with my *insider info* (Kiplinger's) to start choosing the stocks that would earn my portfolio its first millions. One "great value buy" after another graced my cart, but I kept finding myself drawn back to a dark horse. The stock was less than a dollar a share, and the company was described as "going through a major change: it's make-or-break time." I waited through the ever-present internet lag for articles to load about this mail-order movie rental company's new announcement: they were developing a way to blast movies right into your home! I didn't understand the science or how it could possibly work on my computer, which was still on dial-up internet service, but the more I thought about it, the more attractive it was to me. This was mind-blowing sci-fi for 2003; if I couldn't make my first fortune on jetpacks, this was the next best thing. I would be obscenely wealthy *and* a visionary!

I swapped out my entire stock cart for 300 shares and set up the auto-purchase option to grab more whenever my earnings allowed. I knew it was a risky move, though, so before I pressed the final button, I turned to my key advisor on anything and everything—my dad. He wasn't just a brilliant math whiz and ace salesman; he loved me unconditionally. If this idea was as genius as I thought, I wanted him investing with me. I could see our father-son cover of *Fortune* already. (It was stock market–superhero themed.) In the off-chance that I was about to lose my shirt, he'd set me on the right path to protect my investment. He always would make sure I was safe, happy, and very loved.

Over a serious dinner meeting of peanut butter and banana sandwiches, I gave my dad the rundown on my stocks. To my shock and disappointment, his verdict was quick and resolute: "No way. That will never work. Netflix will be bankrupt within a few months."

With a heavy heart, I packed up my jetpack dreams and placed the orders for my good value buys. Netflix was *not* the way to go. My dad said it was a bad investment, so it was a bad investment.

Less than a month later, Netflix started to surge . . . and continued to surge . . . and then surged some more. As we all know, Netflix's crazy movie-streaming service *did* work, and it launched them into the $500-plus-per-share stock market juggernaut they are today.

I'll save you the trouble of doing the math: 300 shares at $1 in 2003 would have been an investment quickly worth $150,000. Not bad for a high school kid, huh? I can't do the retroactive math for how much I would have netted with the standing order to buy more stock, but let's just say that *Fortune* cover wasn't exactly a pipe dream. The safe-bet stocks I actually put my money in went belly up.

I lost some cash, but kept my advisor for managing my time, my calculus homework, and learning to grill a mean sirloin. Even in the Netflix deal, my dad inadvertently provided me with rare and valuable insight: when you're looking for breakthrough advice, your advisors should be focused on your breakthrough—not on you.

We start valuing the advice of parents and friends as soon as we are old enough to comprehend it. Why? Because *it works*. It keeps us alive and afloat. These people want what is best for us in a real, holistic, long-term way—which means they'll almost always champion safe, slow growth than risky innovation. We get tricycles before we graduate to big kid bikes. Even if jumping on a motorcycle could teach us balance, drive, and speed more quickly, no parent in their right mind would swap out their toddler's training wheels for a Harley.

You're grown up now, though, and your breakthrough will require doing new things in new ways. Breakthroughs are risky— and you're going to have to take risks. When you need breakthrough cooperation, you're not always looking for advice from the warm fireplaces, the fresh-baked cookies, or the clean linen that brought you here. You'll need advice from people who are more dedicated to your breakthrough than your safety.

The people closest to you don't necessarily want what's best for your breakthrough; they want what's safest for you. Safe keeps you from your best. The biggest risk you can take is no risk at all; you risk everything when you collaborate only with people who are looking out for you. Seek out wisdom from the wise in the category you need to be wise in, not from the ones who want the best for you.

Many breakthrough teams, particularly in the corporate world, don't have 7.6 billion people to choose from. Sometimes you have to choose from a much smaller team, or it's already chosen for you. As a committed BIOnic leader, it's still your responsibility to follow your intuition and figure out how to utilize the best guidance from your team members in their elite strengths. Don't rely on the hierarchy of the org chart. More than likely, you have someone working above you, beside you, and below you. None of them will be the best person to turn to for advice in every category. In the worst (but seemingly pretty standard) case, you might have a yes-man below you, competition beside you, and someone barking orders above you. Decipher who you can actually form a coalition with: people who will challenge and support you.

What amount of risk do you want in your breakthrough team?

What Are You Hating On?

A lot of people don't like to use the word "hate"—certainly not directed at people. I understand that. Call it what you like (or "strongly dislike"), there are certain things you are repulsed by.

I, for example, *loathe* sauerkraut.

The smell of Swiss cheese is revolting to me.

The only thing worse than eating corned beef is the stench while it cooks.

I wouldn't eat a salad covered with Russian dressing on a bet.

Rye bread? Hard pass.

But the best sandwich in the entire world is a Reuben from Katz's Delicatessen in New York City. Which also might make it the best breakthrough cooperation model BIOnic leaders have.

There's not a single group with more potential for fruitful breakthrough cooperation than the people you just don't automatically gravitate towards. Think of the greatest crew of misfits of all time: the twelve disciples of Jesus. Society either scorned them or ignored them. Matthew, an awkward tax collector despised by his own people, wrote one of the most important books in the Bible. Peter, a simple fisherman with no standing in society, became the rock on which the church was built and the leader of the apostles. Zealots. Thieves. Not exactly the crew you'd imagine being chosen to spread the word of God throughout the world. But like a Reuben, together, they were the perfect combination.

Where's a better place to search for a complementary strength diametrically opposed to yours than someone you just can't imagine having anything in common with? Recognize the misfits, the "flawed," as elite talents the world has not yet embraced. Their loss, your gain! And your closest competition is on a nearly identical mission to you—if you were just a few years behind, that person would probably be one of your heroes. You can go farther together. There is no one person at the top— breakthrough cooperation is understanding that you're building a platform at the pinnacle, and you can make it as large and inclusive as you want.

***

Oh, it was the best of times! I was so in love with Taylor, *and* we were embarking on our first trip together as a couple, *and* it was to Israel! Taylor, travel, tahini—three of the all-time best things (in that order)!

But, sitting in a hotel conference room surrounded by "influencers" the night before we left, while not exactly the *worst* of times, was not great. Not for me. Everyone else, including self-proclaimed introvert Taylor, seemed to be having a great time, chatting and stuffing their faces with pizza.

Was I surprised by my company? No, I knew what I was walking into. Israel Collective was sponsoring this ten-day trip specifically for influencers to learn about the Holy Land and share it with their followers. I'd weighed my options when Taylor told me about it, but that triple-T-threat made the choice obvious. I needed a break from running up and down basketball courts twelve hours a day, but I was here for the tour, the food, and my girlfriend—not to make friends. Not with these people.

I would *never* call myself an "influencer." (To be fair, none of the people in that room would have either. I had fewer than 2,000 Instagram followers; I was clearly Taylor's plus-one.) These YouTubers, rappers, gospel singers, and general social media-ites were not my crowd, to say the least. I had no idea why others would follow them, and no interest in finding out. I plastered a fake smile on my face and deflected conversations as quickly as possible. I was teetering on a thin ledge between obviously rude and very obviously rude. Welcome to the Israel Collective trip.

Finally, Taylor sat down next to me. She put her hands on my knees and said, "David, what's it going to hurt to talk to these people? I know they might not be the people you're used to interacting with, but what if they can offer you a completely different perspective? What's it hurt to try? Someone in this room needs you; act like it's a game of Clue and find out who it is."

That was a dirty trick. Taylor knew I couldn't resist Clue.

I embraced the challenge and began asking people questions like I was trying to get to the bottom of a mystery I put my detective hat on and became *curious*. Curious about others, curious about their stories, curious about what they wanted to get out of this trip. I had so many notes in my head, I could have solved the mystery right then and there on the spot.

As the night went on, I found myself genuinely laughing, smiling, and having a really good time. I actually tried to put my Grinch face back on and act like it wasn't fun. But it was. I was fully embracing the curiosity of looking deep into the people around me. And they were definitely curious. These misfits *were* weird and different . . . and intriguing and inspiring.

We made it to Israel the next day and had an amazing trip, touring the whole country, floating in the Dead Sea, seeing where Jesus was hung on the Cross, climbing mountains in Capernaum, cruising on a boat in the Sea of Galilee, and, of course, eating a lot of high-level hummus. That trip puts all my other vacations to shame.

But what I will remember best from the trip are the people. They were weirdos, for sure. They didn't have that relentless "mission-on-the-mind-24/7" Michael Jordan style I associated with greatness. They were unapologetically different. Total hams. They would get up and give impromptu speeches on the bus, they wrote a lot and took pictures of *everything*, they were always on their phones, and they just seemed to genuinely enjoy and engage with everyone and everything around them, even when they got some disapproving glares. . . .

Okay, they were a lot like me. More like me than a lot of the other "normal" people I usually hung out with. I wasn't a weirdo though, was I?

Well, I gave some of my first public speeches, impromptu, on those buses. And they gave me a lot of great photography tips and explained the economics of "influencing." And I started writing a lot more—so much more that I started my first book when I got home. And obviously I had to keep up my social media accounts when I got home—I couldn't just stop sharing daily life with my Israel Collective friends!

Turns out, there was a weirdo inside of me all along.

You do yourself a disservice if you only surround yourself with like-minded people who look like you, think like you, and act like you. You need the people you would never naturally be drawn to. They can draw the best out of you.

The breakthrough cooperation I shared with the people on that trip launched my career in a whole new direction. They inspired me to take my NBA mindset coaching out into the world. I left for Israel determined not to make friends; I came back with something better—a whole team of breakthrough collaborators.

I make a point now of going to places where I'm not similar to everyone else, from pottery painting studios to hip-hop dance class with my wife. Whenever I feel my face pull into that smelly "Ew, that isn't *me*" grimace, I know I am going to grow from it. And who knows—I might find some more breakthrough cooperation!

Pay attention to people who have the breakthrough confidence to be unabashedly weird. Trust me, you're not the first person who has noticed. The weirdos have needed to battle against people who wanted them to bury their "flaws" their entire lives. They know something about themselves that is too strong to be worn down. There's an elite strength in refusing to hide, an incredibly rare and valuable resource for just about any breakthrough I can conceive of.

What's the rarest complementary misfit strength you're searching for?

***

I hated Drew Hanlen. This goofy twenty-three-year-old kid from St. Louis had no great basketball pedigree, no out-of-this-world on-court talent. He was just another nobody—a nobody who basically every top NBA player looked to for advice and training.

Here I was, twenty-six years old, and this *child* was dominating *my* profession. I wanted the ESPN articles talking about the amazing job *I* was doing for the next up-and-coming NBA All-Star. I wanted agents and teams and players knocking at *my* door to work with *me*. Sure, I had some of that, but *so did Drew*, and that drove me nuts. We were like two competing vanillas in the baking cabinet—and so many people kept reaching for him.

I resented everything Drew had when we were competing neck and neck; imagine how ugly it got once he pulled ahead! For five years, I seethed across the court at my worst enemy. I coached in the NBA for the Brooklyn Nets, trained a ton of players on my own, and my business and reputation grew, but it was never enough. Every time I thought I was one step closer, another top NBA draft pick would crush me with a simple, "I want to thank my trainer, Drew Hanlen, for helping me become the best player I could be," and Drew would take another two leaps ahead on the ladder.

In those moments, I might have traded every one of my successes just to see him fail. I had to just settle for living out my dreams, professionally and personally. In 2019, I married the perfect girl and we moved to the beach in Marina del Rey. Even my apartment complex gym was perfect—until the day I hopped off the treadmill to see Drew.

"What are you doing here?" I snarled.

My mortal enemy accosted me . . . with a giant hug. "Man, it's so great to see you! I've heard about all the awesome work you have been doing with NBA players. So proud of you. We should do something together sometime."

Drew didn't seem to notice I was frozen dead in my tracks as he shared that he'd just moved in so his girlfriend could help him learn to walk again after ACL surgery. The one person in the world I wanted to hate and envy was wounded; I should have felt like all my wishes had been granted. But here he was—kind and encouraging. My heart sank as I realized he'd never once been disrespectful to me or treated me poorly—just the opposite. Drew Hanlen had no idea we were "enemies." He was confident in his skills and talents, and admired mine. He didn't see me as a threat, but as a resource.

I swallowed hard as I actually looked him in the eyes for the very first time and finally saw my greatest adversary reflecting back at me—this crazy jealousy of mine.

The person I thought I had to hate to be successful, my top competition, was actually a great human being and someone I could work together with. Instead of competing, I would be *completing*. That's when it really hit me: collaboration over competition with others is what drives success and joy in the process. I'm definitely not saying you shouldn't compete; competition is a must. But the competition shouldn't be against others. The competition should be against yourself, to fully become the person you were made to be. Don't compete with others, compete alongside others.

Tony Robbins and Dean Graziosi are two uber-successful entrepreneurs and business tycoons in the same market. They can compete against each other for bigger slices of the pie, but they know the pie doesn't have to stay the same size; it can be layers on layers on layers with whipped cream on top. Tony and Dean teamed up and in a one weekend Zoom event during the 2020 crisis that was COVID, they netted over $50 million. Yeah, I'd say it worked to compete *with* and not compete *against*.

It's a simple and startling concept we all learn early in life: if someone wins, someone else loses. If your sister gets the last ice cream bar, you don't. If you want the best swing on the playground, you need to race your classmates there. There's not enough of all the good stuff to go around.

Call it zero sum bias or call it scarcity mentality, this mindset affects high achievers in every field, but it is deeply ingrained in 99 percent of athletes. Competition is one of the very corner-stones of sports. Playing a great game is nice, but winning is everything. Having enough is never enough. *Being* enough is never actually enough. If you are not *the winner*, you are *a loser*.

Of course, if you're around the true geniuses of any game, you know that's not true. Sure, most high achievers have this mentality, but those rare ones who don't shine the brightest. They show us all how it's really meant to be played. Their names are held in the highest regard, their plays are spoken of through generations, their teamwork is legendary. No one remembers the final scores of the games they lose. Through it all, they always win by playing with abundance, kindness, and joy.

That's what stung as I confronted my mortal enemy—I should have known better. Drew's example showed me what I'd truly lost out on over the five years I held this competitive hatred in my heart. My own scarcity mindset had kept me from achieving my truest potential as the coach I was meant to be. I saw limitations and felt bitterness where he saw opportunity and felt joy. He'd known all along that there was plenty out there for everybody, so he'd been able to commit 100 percent to his players. The moment I let him, he looked to collaborate and promote our mutual success and drive even better results for our players—so we could *all* win.

It kills me now to see people who "have it out" for others in their industry, who think they must step on someone else to boost themselves up. It's toxic, which is bad, but you're poisoning yourself worse than you could ever hurt them. Envy others' success, and you will never truly find it. Focus on competition and outdoing your opponent, and you will always be outdone. Selfishly keep everything to yourself, and everything will be kept from you. Embrace completion, collaboration, and connection, and not only will you become more *successful* than you could have imagined, but you will also have peace. Spend the energy you would have wasted on battling an enemy who doesn't even know you hate him on your breakthrough. Recognize, like Drew Hanlen, that your competition is your *greatest* resource—the only people who truly know what you're going through, what you're up against, what you're dreaming of, and what amazing ways you've found to level up. Share with them, and they will share with you.

That's the type of breakthrough cooperation that doesn't stop at the individual level. We are all trying to sell something, whether it's a tangible widget or our personal brand, and none of us are that original. We can compete against a nearly identical brand for the same customers, or we co-populate, like hamburger chains. McDonald's, Burger King, and In & Out all build in the same centralized locations, figuring that people will at least know *the spot* to come when they want a burger. Sure, they each might lose a few customers to the others, but it all works out; a stand-alone McDonald's never does as well as a McDonald's surrounded by the competition.

One is far too small of a number ever to achieve greatness. We need others. Surround yourself with the best in your industry, the best in your organization, and watch as people flock in. One of the most successful sources of breakthrough cooperation is to recruit your competition—not to work for you, but with you and alongside you.

What competitors do you want to cooperate with for your breakthrough?

WHAT DID YOU FORGET?

We've touched on connecting with heroes, family, professionals, co-workers, nemeses, competition, misfits—what *did* we forget?

It's a big one. You're going to be embarrassed you didn't think of it—I was.

Absolutely none of the work you do to connect in breakthrough cooperation matters if you don't cultivate that connection!

I really can't hammer this home hard enough. At best, mindlessly and thoughtlessly networking with people is useless for your breakthrough. It's nearly always actively harmful to your mission.

Don't take advantage of people.

Don't make promises you don't plan on keeping.

Don't believe anyone is too small to be worth keeping your word.

Pay at least as much attention to what you can add to their breakthrough as what you hope they'll contribute to yours.

People remember how you've treated them, *and it weighs way more than you think*.

***

One of my most valuable God-given talents has to be my ability to *connect*. I've always been a social person, but I threw this talent into a networking hyperdrive obsession—and then took it around the globe many times.

As much as I hate the term "networking," I am an absolute master. I pride myself on having a guy for everything in every city. Even for someone with an NBA background, I have a more developed network than many, particularly because of my overseas experience.

So, would it surprise you to learn that my two biggest career setbacks and disappointments are directly related to my strong networking abilities?

When I was looking for the breakthrough to become an NBA coach, the Las Vegas Summer League was my playground.

Late night Tuesday $5 blackjack hands at Ellis Island Casino, early morning pickup basketball runs at Sierra Vista High School, or just bluntly standing in the lobby of Thomas & Mack Center (where all the Summer League games were played) waiting for an NBA team polo to walk through the door, I covered that whole town. I connected with everyone I could find, hoping to make an impression. I amassed a booklet of over fifty NBA business cards for my efforts—but this wasn't an arcade. There was no counter to cash them in for the big prize. I had to hope that at least one of those card owners would give me a shot.

I was half a world away, mentally preparing for another sweaty, smelly, all-day basketball camp in a January-hot summer gym in Melbourne, Australia, when I got word that the Brooklyn Nets wanted to add me to their coaching staff. There was no *one* person that I'd made an impression on—it was simply the fact that my name had kept coming up. Multiple connections, multiple impressions, lots of effort, and I was in.

Stepping on the plane back to the States and into the breakthrough team I'd been dreaming of, I vowed to be the best ingredient they'd ever added. Fast-forward to the end of my first NBA coaching season, and everyone agreed I'd more than meshed—I had taken the Nets' three-point percentage from twenty-eighth in the league to second. I was hot and getting hotter, the zesty pepper of the coaching squad. I was a top shooting coach, and the only thing that could derail me from becoming *the* top shooting coach was the instability of the other ingredients. The Nets were hiring a new head coach, and new head coaches are notorious for coming in and cleaning house, making sure they can bring in all the ingredients they want. I knew I could add heat to any squad—but would the new head coach agree?

On April 17, 2016, the Nets announced former Atlanta Hawks Assistant Coach Kenny Atkinson would take on our top spot, and I was pumped. I hadn't just collected his card at the Las Vegas Summer League—we'd had a full meeting at Starbucks!

I knew Kenny would remember me; he'd been so impressed by my overseas connections that he'd even asked me to look for opportunities for one of his players. Jeremy Lin had played for Kenny, so he even called in and sang my praises. I felt as safe as I could hope to be.

Kenny did a first wave of firings right off the bat, but I didn't hear a word from him—at all. It was a mixed blessing; I was happy to still be on the court with my players, but I felt a little uneasy about the silence. I wasn't off the team, but was I *on* it?

I waited for days to hear from Kenny . . . and I never did. I was still at the gym late one night, breaking down game film for a player, when the GM called me: "Kenny has decided to let you go. You're excused of all duties with the Brooklyn Nets. Please clear out your locker by the end of the day tomorrow and we'll schedule a flight back home for you."

I was rocked to the core. My hopes, goals, and the dreams actively in progress were swept out from under me. Kenny hadn't just rejected the zingy pepper I brought to the mix—he'd actively avoided it.

It took a minute, but I licked my wounds and reminded myself that I wasn't going to be for everyone. None of us are. That's okay. No one has ever had a 100% approval rating in the history of ever. Think about that. So why will you? You aren't the right ingredient for every team, but you are for the *right* team. . .

And then my friend Alex Saratsis became Giannis Antetokounmpo's agent. This "Greek Freak" was one of the best NBA players in the league, and I'd been watching him with interest ever since we'd both been playing professionally in Greece. I'd been playing at the highest level, first division, while Giannis was in second division, so we'd never played each other (it's one of my claims to fame—I played at a level above Giannis!). Of course, he was thirteen at the time and playing professionally against a sea of full-grown men. By the time Giannis made it to the NBA, he'd grown into his seven-foot height; with arms longer than Inspector Gadget's, this kid could now move like a gazelle, handle the basketball like a point guard, and had Kobe's killer mentality. The only flaw left in Giannis's game was an inability to make a shot before the three-point arc.

That's right: the Greek Freak's only flaw was my primary strength. And I was buddies with his agent. The whole world was going to know how I'd impacted the next MVP of the NBA. I was back in, *for sure*.

Alex Saratsis is a top-notch human being: kind, genuinely caring, and very loyal—maybe even to a fault. Alex and I became fast friends through a mutual client. Most agents really don't care about the development of their players; they are more interested in signing on the dotted line of a fat contract. But Alex would take the extra time to call me and talk about his client's improvement, show up at his workouts to watch, and even hop in drills just to show he still had it. (Which he didn't, exactly, but hey, I respected the attempt!) It wasn't just this client, either; Alex was on the hustle, all the time, for each of his clients. Once we were better friends, he even asked me to pull my Australian connections to help another client. I told him I'd make it happen!

When our mutual client went over to play professionally in Germany, he dropped Alex, so I didn't have daily interactions with him anymore. I was hustling with my players and I knew he'd be hustling with his, but when I heard he'd signed Giannis, I was excited to work alongside him again. Together, we'd take the player taking the NBA by storm into the stratosphere!

I whipped out my phone and texted, "Alex, hey man. That's so cool you have Giannis as a client! Great work! I would love to work with him and help him become an elite NBA 3pt shooter."

I watched the three dots bubbling up with a huge grin on my face. Alex was already texting back—in a few short seconds, I would be well on my way to establishing myself as the greatest three-point shooting coach there ever was! All love and respect to Chip Engelland, but I was primed to leapfrog way over him!

Those bubbles burst into Alex's response: "David, I like you. I really do. But I haven't talked to you in over two years, and that is how you are going to reach out? Asking me for the most prized possession in the NBA? Sorry, David."

I dropped my phone, absolutely crushed. How could this be? Wasn't Alex my friend? Didn't I help his former client get better? He'd known my abilities—how could he turn me down?

Sitting on the floor, I remembered Alex had asked me to help him with a connection in Australia . . . but I never actually did it. I hadn't actively worked against him, I just hadn't followed through. At the time, it just didn't move the needle for me, and it was a lot of work to help a player I didn't even know, someone I wasn't getting compensated for. Why *would* Alex help me now? I never went out of my way to *actually* help him. On the surface, we'd worked well together—meaning I'd done my job—but when it really mattered, when he really needed me, I didn't even try to come through. I hadn't been playing with breakthrough cooperation—I'd been a one-note wonder, playing solely for myself. I hadn't even bothered to combine our strengths into something with lasting power.

It cast new light my experience with Kenny Atkinson, too. Yeah, I'd made an impression on him when we met at Summer League, I probably even impressed him with everything I'd worked for, the fifty-plus countries I had traveled to doing basketball camps, the years and years of connecting—but I hadn't followed through and actually helped him. I didn't cultivate the relationship; I didn't join forces with him. Kenny didn't even need to bother telling me himself when he decided we weren't going to work together in breakthrough cooperation at the Nets—I'd already made him feel like I wasn't working in breakthrough cooperation with him long, long before.

Call it connecting, call it networking, call it making an impression—most of us are more eager to be known than to know. We'll take the phone call, send an email, and hand out the business card, but after that, our energetic spark fizzles out. We wait on others to recognize the power of our potential and connect with us.

It doesn't matter how great you think you are. No one cares or remembers your individual needs or wants. If you want to make a lasting impression, a real connection, you *have* to be the cultivator. Breakthrough cooperation isn't about how great you are—it's about showing others how, together, you can make something more complex, powerful, and dynamic.

Connections can just *happen*, but relationships take work. Intentional time is the only way to cultivate a relationship, and you absolutely need true, genuine relationships with the people you want to work in breakthrough cooperation with. What are their hobbies? Do they have kids? Are they a foodie? What makes them think or act the way they do? Embrace this. Take a colleague who loves coffee to the best roastery in town and ask them about their future goals. Take your co-worker who loves authentic Mexican to their favorite restaurant for lunch and talk about their kids. Ask the misfit to take you to the place they like most—your treat!

You don't get a pass on cultivating the connection with your family, either. Time isn't the most important thing you can give to your kids—*intentional time* is. You can be *around* your kids as they play at the park, but yet your nose is stuck in your iPhone, surfing the latest deals on Amazon. Imagine one of your heroes treating you like that after you spent all day anticipating an amazing one-on-one! If you want your kids to leave with the impression you truly care for them, step one is to be there. Step two, *actually* be there. Don't be present and absent at the same time.

Connections are easy—*cultivating* is hard. Don't wait for the other person to do the toughest work—be the one who pushes breakthrough cooperation by figuring out the formula and making the partnership work.

What connections are you forgetting to cultivate?

BREAKTHROUGH COOPERATION KEYS

- Your daily breakthrough success depends more on your relationships than any other factor.
- Weaknesses are just a complements wish list.
- Heroes can contribute to your breakthroughs in many ways.
- The "best" might not be the best for you.
- Compete *with* your competition.
- Embrace the misfits.
- Cultivate your connections.

BREAKTHROUGH COOPERATION TOOL: CULTURAL COMPASS

Before you begin Q2 of your day, take a few minutes to set the Cultural Compass for your breakthrough.

"Culture" is one of those terms that gets thrown around way too often. Ask around for the tangible definition in play, and nine times out of ten, you're going to get the Casablanca Test: Everyone just seems to know it when they see it.

To be fair, culture is complicated. I have been deeply entrenched in some of the worst NBA cultures (coaching with the 2016 Brooklyn Nets, for example), celebrated in the locker rooms with one of the best (the 2019 NBA Champion Toronto Raptors), and have soaked in the knowledge from the architect of the 2009 and 2010 NBA Champion Miami Heat, Erik Spoelstra. I can offer a lot of informed opinions about what makes for great and terrible organizational cultures, but I certainly don't have a failproof cultural formula (yet).

I do know we can't just dictate it. Saying something is our culture doesn't make it real. We can't even just emulate the cultures we admire. Culture is built one day at a time by the ways we act and treat each other, the things we believe, the rules we make and break, the missions we're driving towards, and many other things. But our cultures are never just one person—everyone contributes to the complex blend.

As the BIOnic leader, you're responsible for recruiting the cooperation your breakthrough requires and setting the cultural tone. You can't control it or rush it, but you can steer and influence it. The true essence of your breakthrough culture will be a collaborative effort, but you get to choose the people you're bringing in.

Equipment Required: Pen and Scrap Paper, Email, Notes App—anything you can write on and keep in your pocket

Space Required: Semi-Private to Private, No Distractions

Time Required: <5 Minutes

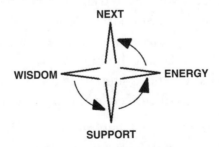

Instructions:

1. Copy some version of the figure below. Yours can be as simple as "+" but just make sure you have four points and the text in order!

2. Starting from Wisdom and moving counterclockwise, take a moment to reflect on each point of your compass and write at least one (but no more than three) answers underneath each point.

   - Wisdom: What external wisdom will benefit your breakthrough today? Do you need advice from a hero who shares your elite strength? A mentor to act as a sounding board and give you feedback? Do you need to swap ideas with a peer? Do you need to dip into books and interviews to collect wisdom you don't have easy access to within your team? There is wisdom all around you—which flavor are you most receptive to today? (Write down what type of wisdom you are searching for and the name of a person who can help you find it.)

   - Support: What is the most important outside support to move the needle on your breakthrough today? Do you need someone with a very specific elite strength in one particular area? Someone to take something off your plate so you can fully use your own elite strengths? Someone to provide emotional support? No successful breakthrough is a solo mission—who are you going to connect with today for the support you need? (Write down what you need support in today and who individually or collectively can provide you with it.)

   - Energy: What energy are you bringing to your breakthrough today, and whose energies will enrich that fuel? Can you amp it up with someone who brings more of your type of energy? Do you need a different type of energy to balance yours out? What type of energy could zap your momentum? Who are you going to connect with and who are you going to shield yourself from to maximize the energy that will move your breakthrough forward today? (Write down what level of energy you need today and who can help bring you that zing!)

- Next: What are you most excited to feel when you reach your breakthrough? Are you anticipating being more energized, relaxed, accomplished, peaceful, strong, victorious, stable, and so on? Thinking about the next level should bring on a complex bouquet of many emotions. Dial it in—which one is most attractive to you right now? To paraphrase the eternal wisdom of Dwayne Johnson, are you smellin' what you're cookin'? Do your answers in Wisdom, Support, and Energy lend you some of that even now? How are you going to bring more of that breakthrough mindset to your day today? (Write down the next big thing on your horizon and someone who has achieved something similar.)

3. Keep your Cultural Compass on you, and refer back to it at the end of Q2. Have you connected with people who met your external Wisdom, Support, and Energy needs?

Chapter 4

Halftime!

Writing my first book, *Pivot & Go*, I almost skipped over morning and evening routines because it felt like starting an NBA training explaining what a basketball is. Everyone must know they need to bookend their days right in order to successfully string together a month of powerful mindset shifts! At the last minute, I included a basic outline—just in case. Turns out a lot of people—including professional athletes, powerful executives, and creative geniuses—hadn't considered the importance of their morning and evening routines *at all*. (I ended up creating several additional tools to help people create, customize, and overlay their ideal routines on their calendars; if you don't have yours optimized yet, you can access those tools on my website, www.davidnurse.com.)

Halftime routines are even more varied and deeply personal than morning and evening routines, but they're crucial to the Breakthrough Blueprint. You feed a lot of new information into your brain in the first half of your day, and you lose 70 percent of new information within twenty-four hours of learning it if you don't find a way to capture it. You'll start off Q3 and the second half of your day dedicated to outward action. You are essentially working on another muscle group entirely, so you need a halftime break to find your rhythm and make sure the important new intel you've earned sticks.

There is a reason nearly every sports game has a halftime or an intermission. It's not just for resting, recovering, and recharging; it's for rescheming the game plan, reassessing the offensive attack, and realigning the defensive strategy. Halftime is about taking yourself off the court—not out of the game—so your brain can consolidate your experiences, conscious thoughts, and independent information, and prepare to react and interact with the environment in a new way.

Games aren't won at the start, and they aren't necessarily lost at the end. What happens during the in-between determines everything. I have every tool you need to build out your customized breakthrough halftime online; check those out, and schedule ten to twenty minutes of uninterrupted time between your Q2 and Q3 to dominate your halftime and win your day.

No matter what your customized optimal breakthrough halftime plan looks like, one element is universal: you need to choose your second.

HALFTIME TOOL: CHOOSE YOUR SECOND

I originally developed this simple tool to harness the mental and physical talents of NBA players who stressed over the shot clock. It was so effective that I adapted it for general use—we all need a rallying moment. I check my own several times each day, and I'm amazed at the clarity it provides. If you walk away from today with only this tool, you will still be an immensely better worker, a clearer thinker, and a more centered person. And it's so simple!

Equipment Required: Clock or Watch with a Second Hand

Space Required: Anywhere

Time Required: <3 Minutes

Instructions:

1. Choose a number between 1 and 24; that is the second within each minute that belongs entirely to you. That is the second in which you have the optimal breakthrough confidence, in which you have the strongest resolve to serve your team and the world with your strengths and talents.

2. Every time throughout Q3 and Q4 that you feel yourself slipping or stressing, smile, focus your eyes on the second hand, and take a breath. Collect yourself. Wait for your chosen second.

3. When your second strikes next, begin again, fresh from your strongest mental space. No matter what you are doing, it takes less than a minute to solidify yourself as a truly clutch player.

CHAPTER 5

Q3: Seeing Where: Breakthrough Service

In the first half of your day, you intentionally develop your two greatest breakthrough resources—yourself and your team. Just finding breakthrough confidence in your elite strengths and building breakthrough cooperative relationships with your complementary teammates will take you further than most people can even imagine.

But you aren't most people, you are BIOnic—a Breakthrough Impact Optimization expert!

In Q3, you will channel your developing strengths and resources in order to answer the where: where are you needed? You pivot away from focusing inward so you can be of greater service to the world. You still have the opportunity to test and exponentially improve yourself and your team, but now you'll gain insight into issues that your breakthrough can solve. You'll sharpen your vision of how your breakthroughs can impact the world—and where the world needs that impact.

Vision is the Q3 sense, and the one we value most as a society. We talk and think about sight more than any other sense, and we highly value the information we see. Even the language we use around sight is elevated—we are perceptive, keen-eyed visionaries with colorful ideas who reflect, and see clearly with foresight. Seeing is believing! Avoid tunnel vision at all costs. No one operates well with blinders on. What we see is what we know.

It's true that what we see *is* the majority of what we know. Our eyes can process over 36,000 pieces of information each hour, and our eye muscles are the fastest in our bodies. Our eyes are the second most complex organs we have.

But we also have some blind spots—literally. We never see objects themselves; we only see how light reflects off of them. We take in the information contained in those reflections, flip it upside down, read it, and then flip it right side up again so we can understand it. There aren't any light-sensitive cells where our optic nerves connect to our retinas though, so the pictures we're taking of the world are always incomplete. Our brains help us out by filling in information from how things "should" be—based on the previous knowledge we have, the different perspectives we've gotten, and our ideas of what we can expect. But we never actually have a clear picture, and those blind spots frequently work against us. Inattentional blindness (an inability to perceive an unexpected object in our field of vision) and change blindness (failing to see when an object has obviously changed or moved in an unexpected way) are more than just dangerous on the road— they're dangerous to our breakthroughs! If we don't put real effort into getting multiple perspectives of the world, coming up with more snapshots to fill in our missing data and correcting our ideas of how things "should" be, we risk having breakthroughs that can't make the impact we want them to—or even worse, make the wrong impact altogether.

Switching your lens to breakthrough service in Q3 means more than just doing nice or selfless things for others. It is a commitment to understanding the needs of the world from different perspectives, to putting yourself in others' shoes as you help them. Service doesn't always show up in the stats sheet, but it's what leaves a legacy.

The biggest breakthroughs are recorded in history books and passed down through future generations. All of the "greats," from George Washington to Martin Luther King Jr. to Harriet

Tubman, have their deeds recorded, but these achievements, these breakthroughs that we talk about—they're just shorthand. They're just the only way we can truly talk about incredible people doing impossible things. And without fail, they achieve these breakthrough by-products by genuinely pouring themselves into others.

Service is the lasting legacy of the truly groundbreaking and truly great. Every hero throughout history has changed the game in service to others. Finding answers for "where are you needed?" is absolutely essential—you'll not only hit your "hows" time and time again, but you'll create something impactful with your breakthroughs.

Service is about sharing the best parts of you with everyone around you, about helping them tap into the skills they didn't even know that they had, and about identifying roadblocks and opportunities for them. It is the breakthrough confidence you earn and exude by making the world an incredible place with every single one of your actions and then offering more. It's about seeing where your strengths are needed. It's about committing yourself, your leadership, your team, and your future to making others stronger and better.

Yes, you'll be gifting the world—but these aren't the easy, polite, impersonal gifts you may be used to giving. Breakthrough service often feels great, but there will be acts of breakthrough service that are difficult, challenging, and feel counterproductive. No matter what, you'll be gaining an incredible amount of information from the world to inform your own breakthroughs.

WHERE IS THE CHALLENGE?

Who doesn't love to be liked?!

Sure, some people seem to get a huge kick out of being feared—bosses who make their employees dance for their approval, drill sergeant personalities who bark orders, strict parents who withhold affection until everything is done just right. I'm sure you've even run into people who seem to actively court being disliked—drivers who go out of their way to cut you off in traffic, waiters who unpleasantly rush you out the door, the guy who always throws sharp elbows in pickup basketball games. But I have to imagine that even those people love to be liked by *someone*.

Most of us don't start our days committed to making people dislike us. A lot of us actually bend over backwards to be liked! We want to be buddies with everyone—our co-workers, our team, our kids. We're nice to strangers, acquaintances, and our nearest and dearest alike. I think most people who've met me would say I'm a nice person!

Sorry to break it to you, I'm not.

I'm *kind*. I'm a kind person who tries to be nice whenever possible—but when the kind thing and the nice thing are different, I'm going to choose to do the kind thing.

Breakthrough service is recognizing that kindness is more important than niceness. You serve people best by helping them grow, and they grow most by being challenged. Loving people unconditionally doesn't mean giving them unconditional approval—it means challenging and supporting them. They might not like you for it, but that's okay. It's not about how you feel—it's about what you can give. Breakthrough service might require you to give up being liked! Concentrate your acts of breakthrough service on helping others see themselves better, not on how they see you.

***

To the birds roosting in the sky-high rafters, the scene on the court must have looked like a ripple of happiness. The outermost edge of the ring was composed of the adoring fans—my class-mates, my family, and my entire community had come out to watch the Iowa high school varsity championship game. Regardless of the final tally, the athletes on both teams had con-ducted themselves with honor through a season of fierce compe-tition, and win or lose, they would return home with even more love for the game. As the final buzzer pierced the air, the tightest circle formed in the very middle of the court; my teammates, the Fighting Dutchmen, spent the last ounce of the adrenaline that had carried us through our title win in sheer jubilation.

There was just one disturbance in the celebration ripple, one dark spot of brittle energy that wasn't swept up. As a fresh-man, I should have been the most honored to share in this cham-pionship victory. But I didn't feel like a part of the team. I felt like a punching bag. I yearned to be told how good I was, but my coaches and teammates had thrown me into the fire, hoping to forge me into the player they thought I could be. After a season of constant criticism, I just felt fragile.

A few months after that game, my family moved from Pella, Iowa, to Kearney, Missouri. From one Midwest town to another, I wasn't expecting a huge culture shock, but Kearney was a whole different world for me. I was only a sophomore, but I was crowned as the go-to guy from the moment I rolled onto the court. Suddenly, I was coddled—the coach's favorite player. I jumped into my new role as the spoiled prince with a vigor that I had never shown in Pella, lording it over my teammates on the court and my fellow students in the classroom. I sat behind the desk of the history teacher (my basketball coach) with one eye on the sports page of the newspaper and one eye on my studying class-mates, delighting in their envy of my elevated position.

Nothing about my game had changed between Pella and Kearney, and I had zero motivation to make any improvements. I was a huge talent in this particular pond. What more could I need?

I finished my star season at Kearney and rode into the summer AAU league in Kansas City on a cloud of best-player buzz. In the gym at Central High School for the first time, I graced my soon-to-be AAU teammates with a game of two-on-two. Sure, I threw lazy passes. No, I didn't hustle back on defense. If the past year had taught me anything, it was that my good enough was certainly good enough.

But instead of getting love from Coach Isaac Chew, I got a mouthful. Chew *ripped* into me: "What the hell are you doing, David? Who do you think you are? You say you want to play D1? Well, you sure as hell ain't D-anything playing like that."

Doesn't he know? I'm one of the top players in Kansas City. He can't talk to me like that!

Coach Chew burst the bubble Kearney had spent a year building around me, and I felt the Pella flames creeping up on me all over again. I couldn't go back to being berated every day. I couldn't go back to the constant criticism. If my dream really required being torn apart, bit by bit, every moment, did I even want it? Would there be enough left of me at the end to appreciate it? I spent the rest of the practice in the VIP room of my one-man pity party.

When Coach Chew pulled me into his office after practice and sat me down, I braced myself for the wrath and prepared to hop out of the fire. I'd go back to Kearney. I'd dump my D1 dreams. I'd be the hometown hero through high school, and just try to live in that bubble of praise for as long as possible. If a breakthrough into bigger leagues required the searing clarity of constant criticism, that just wasn't for me.

I watched Chew open his mouth and expected a flame-thrower; what I got were words of uplifting love: "David, you are going to be a great player. You really are. And I think the sky's the limit for you. Not only that, but you are going to be a great leader. If I let you off the hook for being less than you are capable of, I'm doing you a disservice. I'm going to challenge you, and it's going to help you grow. But know it is all out of love."

I was completely stunned. The ways the Pella coaches challenged me had made me a better player, but the price was hating myself. The way the Kearney coaches coddled me made me love myself more, but the price was it downgraded the way I played the game. In a single day, this Kansas City coach had given me clarity into the blueprint for my breakthrough—not just for my basketball career, but for my entire life. He became my first model for the key breakthrough service lens: challenge *and* support. Constant praise and constant criticism each make us fragile in different ways—but they both make us fragile. True breakthrough leadership is building up strength in others by applying both as they are needed.

Isaac Chew called me after every high school game to challenge me on what I could do to improve my game, my teammates, and my overall character. He supported me when each of the three colleges I was hoping to play for informed me on the same exact day that they were going with the other guy instead. He challenged me as the captain of the Western Illinois Leathernecks. Even today, he is there with clarity and vision to serve my breakthroughs as a speaker, challenging and supporting me as each situation calls for. I don't know what I did to deserve the breakthrough service of Isaac Chew in my life, but I wouldn't be where I am without him.

I challenge myself to provide the same breakthrough service to others that Isaac Chew provides to me: love 'em to the core with support, and challenge 'em to the max. If you only support, you become a yes-man. If you only challenge, you become a drill sergeant—and eventually people just tune you out. The growth combo of the right amount of challenge and the right amount of support isn't an exact formula or recipe. It's more difficult, it's always changing, it requires more attention. It requires true service.

Humans struggle to provide this breakthrough service, but it's instinctive to many other animals. The elegant, graceful giraffe is my wife's favorite animal, and while I've had many opportunities to admire their dappled coats and elongated necks, I never truly understood her appreciation for them until I saw their parenting techniques.

When a baby giraffe is born, the mother kicks the baby to the ground. And when the baby gets back up, she makes sure it goes down again. And again. And again.

Sounds brutal, right?

The mother giraffe is protecting the baby from lions. She's teaching it how to get back up quickly on its own because if she didn't, the baby would unquestionably become a gourmet lunch for Simba and his tribe.

Coddling people feels good. It feels loving. They feel safe and secure and cared for, and you get to bask in the glow. But when you truly care about serving others, about helping them grow, and about helping them achieve breakthroughs by learning more about the world, there will be more situations that call for *challenge and support*. Driving the best out of others by pushing them slightly outside of their comfort zone might not make you the instant favorite, but if you're also there to pick them up when they're defeated, they're much safer, stronger, and more secure. Part of the breakthrough service is knowing you have to create superheroes all around you, rather than building yourself up to be everyone else's savior.

As a reformed "wants everyone to like me" person myself, I pay a lot of attention to the elite performers who haven't embraced the breakthrough service of challenging and support- ing other people. It's obvious that when we prioritize being liked by people over doing what's best for them, that's not a selfless service—that's us being all wrapped up in ourselves. But the dirty secret behind elite performers who always take the biggest, most difficult tasks off anyone's plate? They're usually hiding from their own big, nasty task. They're coddling themselves as much as anyone.

People tell you to "eat the frog," to tackle the hardest things first so you face your fears before breakfast. It's the idea that you should just push through with the sole purpose of surviving. That's all wrong! The thing you are dreading—you need to get so much more out of that than just surviving. Consider the task you're dreading. An email, a phone call, or a meeting that you'd even schedule a root canal to avoid. Don't be shy, we've all got them. But commit to doing it in breakthrough service to yourself and your team.

It's a complete mindset pivot, but when we pay close attention, those opportunities we dread are some of the best opportunities we have to act in true breakthrough service. Be kind, not nice, to yourself and everyone around you.

Where are you being nice instead of kind?

WHERE DOES ASKING GET ANYONE?

Are you two-faced?

I always thought "two-faced" was a terrible insult. It wrapped so many traits no one wants into one package: Sneaky. Untrustworthy. Duplicitous.

In Japanese culture, they also talk about having two faces— the *omote* and the *ura*. *Omote* is the face you wear in public, the person you are to most of the world. *Ura* is the face you wear with your closest friends and family.

Learning a little about the Japanese concept of "two-faced," it didn't seem like a bad thing. Of course I had an *ura*—who isn't more vulnerable with the people they are super close to? I'll express my doubts and innermost thoughts to my wife that I'd never dream of spilling in line at the grocery store. I'll ask my friends personal questions and for big favors, and I expect them to do the same with me—but it would feel odd with an acquaintance, much less a random stranger. Even if we love everyone, we love the people we feel safest with on an entirely different level. We are committed to giving them more, so we feel comfortable asking for more. That just makes sense.

But I kept thinking about my *omote*. There are so many questions we're not supposed to ask people. It's just not polite to pry. And who wants to be seen as an "askhole"—the type of person who requests huge favors from people who don't owe them anything? The whole thing made me so uncomfortable—so I knew I needed to try it out.

Turns out, asking those *omote*-level questions and favors can be a huge breakthrough service. If we want to have breakthroughs we haven't had before, we're going to need to do things differently. If we want to know what's possible, we're going to have to dig deeper, share and ask more than we're comfortable with—not just of ourselves, not just of our team, but of the whole world.

***

When I was a kid, there was only one group of people I looked up to more than NBA players—famous world explorers. No high school counselor was going to sign off on my plan to discover new lands—that career path was only open to astronauts and deep-sea divers. But little did they know that when they signed off on my plan to play basketball, that plan took me everywhere. For six years, I slept mostly in cars, buses, and airports, and lived my waking hours in the strange new cities and countries in between. I made friends and learned how to communicate in languages I'd never even heard. I spent more time exploring the world than on any basketball court, and I found that with the right glasses, every person and every place contained a multitude of undiscovered lands.

Lots of people love to travel, but very few explore. I can wait impatiently for a decent Groupon deal for SpaceX tickets to Mars, but I can also easily discover new worlds without ever even pulling out my passport. One of the most intensive trips I've ever taken was with Landry Fields, and we never even had to leave the historic Pauley Pavilion practice court. The former superstar NBA player and current NBA GM didn't have to take any interest in me, but he did—and taught me a critical component of breakthrough service.

I was consulting for UCLA basketball, and Landry was just one of seven different NBA scouts who all came to watch this practice and evaluate future potential players. The six other scouts sat in stony silence, scribbling in their notebooks, *listening* intensely to Coach Steve Alford as he ran the players through a variety of offensive and defensive drills.

"David, right? Can I ask you a few questions?" Landry asked.

I was startled—he'd not only broken the scout-silence, but he knew my name!

"What do you think of the players?"

I answered with something very generic: "They're great kids, working hard, and I really enjoy being around them." A complete BS answer—not that it wasn't true, but it was about as deep and useful as commenting on the weather to a stranger. It was a surface-level interview answer.

"Is there anything that stands out to you about *that* player?" Landry asked, pointing to Lonzo Ball.

Lonzo was the top-rated player in the entire country at that time; anyone who'd ever touched a basketball knew he was going to be a top five pick in the upcoming NBA draft, and most likely the number one overall selection. I had to wonder if Landry was cut out for scouting if he didn't already have a full stat-sheet on Lonzo.

"Yeah, I love him, he's got great vision, he really knows how to put his teammates in the best position possible to succeed. He's got a bright future ahead of him in the NBA, for sure," I responded.

"Sure," Landry said, "he's special, but what makes him different from every other player in the draft? Who is he as a person? What is he like off the court, and in the locker room? How does he treat the walk-on players on the team? Who is he at the core? I already know he's the player that everyone gets to see nightly on the *SportsCenter Top Ten* plays."

Wow, Landry wasn't messing around. No other scouts were asking these types of questions. He wanted to know Lonzo inside and out.

So I told him about how Lonzo reached out to a walk-on who was going through a tough time with his family. How he was the player who made sure the team hung together off the court. How he helped the manager fold the towels in the locker room after practice. How Lonzo genuinely cared about others—on the basketball court and off.

Landry smiled. That was what he was looking for—that's what he'd been digging for. He'd been searching for the information and clarity that no stats sheet or highlight reel contained. Landry wasn't just willing to keep asking questions until he found the unexplored areas—he listened with value. He made me feel valued, but he continued to contribute by asking clarifying questions while I answered.

Far too often, we avoid asking questions because either we don't want to hear the answers, or we are too consumed with ourselves. When we do ask the question, we listen passively, saying nothing and waiting for the answers. Breakthrough service is being actively *curious* in others, and actively asking questions to find out everything about them. We're in good company; Socrates was so famous for teaching through questioning that we still use his method today. The Gospels record Jesus asking 307 questions; in comparison, he was asked 183 questions, and only gave definitive answers to 3. One of the greatest leaders of all time asked more questions than he answered. Talk about the definition of being curious! Our breakthrough might not be as simple as asking clarifying questions, but it will matter greatly. It is the difference between chatting about the weather or exploring new lands; it's helping others to understand the hidden depths within them so that they can break through.

Where are you while you're listening, and where are your questions?

***

Brett Hagler grew up like me, infatuated with basketball and determined to make it big in the game. Unfortunately, he also shared my issues with gravity. Brett was twenty-four when he realized that no matter how hard he lived and breathed basketball, he was never going to reach the next level—that gravity was always going to hold him down.

Brett was a competitor through and through, and without basketball, he had no idea how he was going to fill that void. Basketball had been his driving force for so long that he hadn't even really developed any other passions. That is, other than watching *The Jetsons*.

On a mission for a new life purpose, Brett decided to explore a part of the world he'd never been to and help people who were in a worse jam than he was in. He linked up with a nonprofit and hopped on a flight down to Haiti, where the 2010 earthquake had years earlier destroyed thousands of homes, and disaster relief charities had quickly responded. Brett stepped off the plane and saw the sea of tents, volunteers, and families without homes, and knew that something was very wrong. He was expecting to see pain—after all, he'd come here with dreams to help alleviate it. As a highly empathetic person, he wasn't even surprised to be overwhelmed by it. But there was something more here, and Brett became determined to figure out what it was.

The first issue was easy enough to pinpoint. It was 2013, three years after the earthquake, but there were still thousands of families living in tents, unable to safely rebuild their homes and their lives. Brett's group was here to build a single home; the math just didn't add up. How many hundreds of trips, thousands of volunteers, and countless hours would it take to give *all* these people back their homes?

Brett was here to be of service, but he quickly realized he wanted to be in Haiti in *breakthrough* service. So he started asking questions. He questioned the prevailing wisdom about the costs of construction, the economics of volunteering, and the pace of building. He asked questions to families in the tents, and actively listened as they answered with what they wanted and the ways in which they wanted to be empowered. Armed with their answers, his empathy, and the fierce sense of competition that he developed in basketball, and even his childhood love for *The Jetsons*, he headed home to grow his breakthrough service.

Brett's mission quickly spread from Haiti to several other countries; he set out to build entire communities in ways no one had seen done before, while simultaneously building a culture of empowerment philanthropy within them. He asked, and people told him that there was real power in home ownership, especially when they never thought they could afford one. So he cut the cost of making the houses in half in order to help the people who really need to purchase their own. He leaned on the innovative elements he loved watching on *The Jetsons* to come up with the idea of building homes faster using 3D printing! He made philanthropy a realistic career with an attractive salary, rather than sticking to the limited mindset that it's only a career path for those who are already independently wealthy. He constructed a transparent donation system so that people can be confident that their funds are going directly towards the projects they support.

To date, the charity that Brett founded, New Story, has constructed over three thousand homes in over thirty communities and counting, providing an awe-inspiring and incredible service. But I'd say his breakthrough service started long before when he decided to actively listen by questioning—and without this breakthrough service ability, the rest of what he accomplished would have never happened.

When we let go of the status quo and actually get our hands dirty with the problem, we are able to see the solutions that were there all along. We must look outside the box, yes, but first we must look from the inside out.

Where are you sympathetically nodding instead of asking how you can help?

***

The earthquake shook my body like a ragdoll, and I was having trouble standing. Unfortunately, I was all alone. Not in the room—no, there were a couple thousand people in there with me, although I was the only one up on the stage. But my earthquake was internal, so if I lost my footing and started flopping around on the ground, it was going to cause quite a stir. I hadn't seen any keynote speeches before, but I was pretty certain I was supposed to stay upright.

Here I was, the keynote speaker for the Nestlé annual kick-off. I was the hired gun to spark not only this one event, but set the tone for their entire year, and I hadn't even *seen* a single key-note speech before, much less given one.

After my first book was published, my friend Paul asked if he could bring me into his office at Nestlé to motivate his team and drop some wisdom. I assumed he wanted me to do the type of team and individual coaching I had been doing for years, so I quickly agreed to doing it—but then my eyes widened as he started describing what he envisioned I would do. Speeches. Big speeches. I'd been toying with pursuing a speaking career, but it was all very much in the daydream phase. I had no track record, no speaking highlight reel, no sold-out arenas, and definitely no hot coal gimmick. Heck, I didn't even have a speech. I laughed it off into the "someday" folder—or I thought I did. Paul, being the excellent member of my breakthrough team that he was, apparently didn't hear it that way.

A month later, I got a call from the person at Nestlé in charge of vetting potential speakers. I was surprised, but I wasn't about to turn down a possible breakthrough opportunity—particularly since Paul had put his own neck on the line by asking his employer. So I figured that having the conversation never hurts, right?

Well, it became pretty obvious a few minutes in that I was already *way* in over my head. The very first step of the vetting process was a nonstarter for me: they needed speaking videos. Of course they did. Problem was, I'd never even spoken to a live audience, much less been filmed doing so. I couldn't have film from events that never happened. I thanked the man on the other line of the phone, and placed the idea back up on the "someday" shelf.

Except my breakthrough team was already coming together around me, sweeping that shelf clean. Paul believed I could do it—he'd put his professional reputation on the line to recommend me to his company. When I told my wife I needed film, she knew exactly what to do and immediately dialed up her acting coach. Of course I could have film—we'd rent out a local church stage, grab a few friends, and with a couple of quick costume changes, we could make some Hollywood magic. The speaker who'd never spoken could have a dozen clips of himself in front of adoring audiences. Late into the night, my editor and I came up with sound clips for speeches that didn't exist—but they sure sounded cool. Less than twenty-four hours later, I had an awesome speaking reel. Shoot, I almost fooled myself into thinking I was a real-life professional speaker.

I hesitated before I submitted it to Nestlé, but I knew I owed it to my team. It was the longest shot in the world, anyway. Competition in the speaking field is fierce; by the time you get up to Fortune 500 engagements, you've got references, relationships, awards, and all that "speaker" other stuff. But I had my breakthrough confidence, so I was willing to lay down my one-story ranch of cards next to Taj Mahals like those of Tony Robbins. I'd probably never get a callback, but I couldn't refuse making the ask—not after so many people had poured into me.

When I got a call from a Minnesota number asking for Keynote Motivational Speaker David Nurse, I was caught off-guard, but quickly recovered: "Yes, that is me," I answered confidently. The conversation lasted about thirty minutes and primarily consisted of me making promises I thought a motivational speaker would make. At the end, the man asked me the final question—the only one that really choked me up: "So, what's your speaking fee?"

I talk every day, all day, for free! Shoot, I'll pay Nestlé to allow me to do this talk! Wait, what talk? I don't have a talk!

I opened my mouth, prepared to admit that I'd taken this game as far as I could. As much as I'd love to be a bona fide "askhole," I just didn't have it in me. Nothing had ever been just given to me before; I've always had to earn my spot (even if I had to earn it on the spot!).

But a sudden flash of inspiration shot out of my brain, straight through my open mouth, and I spouted out a truly ludicrous number.

Without hesitation, the man on the other end of the phone said, "Great, we'll send the contract over tomorrow."

Wait, what? I was in. I was not only in—I would be able to pay my breakthrough team back for their time and belief in me. I was officially a keynote motivational speaker. Now, I just had to figure out what the heck I was going to talk about.

Luckily, I had an ace up my sleeve—my book editor and right-hand partner in crime. She helped me find the flow for my first book, *Pivot & Go* (as well as the book you are currently reading!); and she helped me craft up the soundbites for the amazing speeches-that-never-actually-happened in my speaking reel. Together, we could scheme up *something* on breakthroughs, since that was Nestlé's theme for the year. Starting with just the title—*The Breakthrough Blueprint*—and an aspirational tagline—"How to turn *happy accidents* into regularly occurring breakthroughs"—we worked tirelessly, day after day, until we had something so authentic, tight, and true that we thought it might even make a great book someday. . . .

Then, I set to burning it into my brain. But it wasn't happening. I am about the worst memorizer you can imagine. I can't even remember my wife's phone number, let alone an entire speech. I practiced the talk in my head while walking around a Tokyo basketball court as the Japanese basketball team that I consulted for awaited each game's tip-off. I had one week to go, and no capacity to do it. Frustrated, distraught, and stressed to the max, I announced to myself I was calling Nestlé and telling them to find someone else.

But my team would have none of that. My editor, my wife, and her acting coach decided they'd do anything to make sure I saw this through—including listening to me stumble through the talk 163 times. I'm sure I could have stretched it to 164—heck, I'm sure they would have patiently sat through it 164,000 times—but at 163 (yes, I recorded the exact number; confidence is in the preparation!) I didn't just sound okay—I sounded like the actual, real-life motivational speaker I'd claimed to be.

I became obsessed. Possessed. But that's what you have to do in order to learn a new skill in hyper-speed time. That was a personal breakthrough I found: to become *outstanding*, we must go through a period of obsession. A period of completely blocking out the chatter and noise surrounding us so that we can pour every ounce of our being into the new skill. We don't have to go at this pace forever, but to be *elite* at anything, we must run parts of our life marathon in Usain Bolt sprints. I couldn't have done it for myself—but in service to my team, I could make sacrifices and run faster than the speed of light.

"Colorful" by Jukebox the Ghost blared through the speaker system as I picked my body up from the chair in that Nestlé auditorium—literally forcing myself up to the stage. I stood in front of an audience of Nestlé's highest performers and world-changing minds. It was on.

After what felt like five minutes, I glanced down at the clock and realized that fifty minutes had actually whizzed by—and so had I. I wrapped up my talk to a standing ovation from the sea of motivated and inspired Nestlé employees.

I had done it. The man who hired me bounded up to the stage, gave me a big hug, and said, "Thank you, you crushed it!" I wandered down into the audience as multiple people came up to shake my hand and tell me it was the best talk they'd watched in the eighteen-year run of the event. Better than even some of the world-renowned speakers who had formally graced the stage—even David Goggins, who spoke the year before.

If I hadn't put aside my personal pride and fear of looking like an "askhole," I would have let down my whole team. What looked easy on stage—hitting all my points (and having points to hit!), landing all my jokes, even nailing the most natural-looking gestures, steps, and movements—was the cumulation of tireless, around-the-clock obsession, preparing for an opportunity that could change my life. And it wasn't just my tireless efforts; it took a village of people who poured into me because they believed in my breakthrough. I was the one carrying the baton to the finish line, but if I'd refused to ask in the first place, I wouldn't have just crushed my own opportunity—I would have also thrown away their efforts as well. Asking wasn't a selfish act—it was a breakthrough service.

We've all felt that regret wondering why we didn't just ask *that* question. Why couldn't we pull ourselves together to ask for that one thing we wanted so badly—even if we didn't necessarily "deserve" it. What was holding us back? Were we afraid the answer wouldn't be the one we wanted? Were we afraid we would be laughed at, ridiculed, made to feel less than, or publicly squashed like an ant? Probably a mixture of all of the above.

Plain and simple, a question unasked is a question unanswered—and when you're working on behalf of a breakthrough team, finding answers is always a service. Ever since my Nestlé experience, I've committed to performing the breakthrough service of asking.

Asking isn't selfish—it's a breakthrough service. The answer to everything you are looking for might just be one question away. Asking the question doesn't mean you need to accept and act on every piece of advice you get; it means getting more snapshots so you can put together a more accurate vision. We often don't want to listen to our parents, our spouses, or even our kids, because we want to be right and in charge. Being right is *actually* about seeking from your team and making the most informed decision together. Without asking for help and guidance, you will never know. Shed your pride in being right and ask. When you are in the midst of a storm in your life, there is only one way to right the ship: *ask!*

Take the first step, ask the question. The second step could be just the breakthrough you have been searching for!

Yes, of course, insist on getting what you deserve: the promotion, the pay raise, the new challenges. You know the tireless work you have put in and you know you deserve to be compensated and appreciated for it. Ask the question, not out of selfishness, but out of wanting to better others around you in an act of breakthrough service. Tell your boss it's time you take on a bigger challenge, a bigger opportunity to help drive the culture and the entire company to higher heights. It's actually selfish *not to ask* when you know you can empower and help others through the promotions, opportunities, and requests you can use to further their lives. Don't think of it in terms of "deserving"—think of it in terms of how you can use moving forward as an act of breakthrough service to others.

Where is the opportunity you "deserve," and where can you do better for others by asking?

WHERE SHOULD YOU SHOW UP?

Do you consider yourself a charitable person? Do you perform acts of charity? Do you contribute time, money, and other personal or professional resources to charity?

Not complicated, right? I think most of us consider ourselves (or would like to consider ourselves) charitable. We want to make the world a better place—that's one of the key drivers for pursuing breakthroughs, after all. And we recognize that we are blessed with talents, strengths, and resources that others do not have.

But who is worthy of your charity? Would you be comfortable receiving the charity you give? I think these questions are more complicated and difficult for us to answer. Thinking deeply about charity makes us uncomfortable.

Acting in breakthrough service requires us to acknowledge that we all have different elite strengths—and no person on Earth has them all. You are both more *and* less fortunate than everyone you will ever meet. Be charitable with relentless consistency. Show up everywhere ready to contribute your elite strengths. Approach everyone with charity and respect, from the CEO to the janitor, your competitor, and the person without a home. You are offering the best of yourself to help them breakthrough; provide the breakthrough service of approaching it from their perspective.

Please keep giving to charities, please keep being charitable. But in all areas of your life and your breakthrough service, close the gap to understand better how you can contribute to others' breakthroughs. The charitable spirit is at the heart of all breakthrough service, regardless of the circumstance.

Keep showing up. If you are not allowed to serve by doing it your way, ask what you can do to help. Always show up as the person who wants to act in breakthrough service. Maybe you'll get the chance to apply your breakthrough solution to the problem. Maybe you'll learn more about what the actual pain points are, and how different they were from your outsider perspective. Maybe you'll earn trust. Maybe you'll be part of the breakthrough. Expand the breakthrough possibilities by just simply showing up.

***

Coming to the office day after day might not seem like an incredible act of breakthrough service to many—but it should.

Edwin Arroyave's family emigrated from Columbia when he was just a toddler, but they weren't living the American Dream. Two weeks after settling in Glendora, California, the federal authorities raided their beautiful new home. The feds kept coming back, deeply suspicious that Edwin's parents were involved in drug trafficking for the Medellín Cartel—and they weren't without reason. After the fourth raid, Edwin's father was arrested. Knowing he would be incarcerated for years, Edwin's father told the boy he needed to take care of his family.

So Edwin went out to find a job as soon as he could, but he was young, painfully shy, and overly anxious. He went to interview after interview, failing them all. But he kept showing up. Day after day after day.

Edwin's interview at L.D. Services was a particular flop. He had sweated through his shirt, and his mind went blank each time the interviewer asked him a question. He stumbled over words and forgot some altogether. Not an auspicious launch for a telemarketing gig.

As he left the interview, he walked out the door past a man who abruptly stopped him. When the man said, "When are you starting, kid?" Edwin told him that he wasn't—that he'd failed the interview.

But in a flash of bravery, Edwin mustered the courage to ask the man for his help. And the man replied, "I have a job for you."

For three years, Edwin continued to show up to that job. He didn't only do his work, he did more than was even asked of him. He would wait outside to be available for anyone who needed help. If a salesman needed a hand, he would lend it; if an employee needed a coffee run, he would bolt to the nearest Starbucks. Whatever they would allow him to do, he did.

Edwin spent three years continually showing up, always ready to work. And ready to work harder if the opportunity presented itself.

And then one day, it happened. Five employees showed up late after a long night of partying, and the boss fired them all on the spot—the same five employees who stood between Edwin and the next level. He was immediately promoted, despite being too young and too inexperienced.

Edwin went on to start his own home security company, now worth upwards of $100 million, marry the amazing and stunning Teddi Mellencamp (daughter of rock legend John Mellencamp), and raise three adorable, full-of-life kids. But what really grabs me is that Edwin showed relentless consistency in showing up and serving in the ways that the company needed—not showing up and doing whatever he thought was best, but listening to the company's pain points and implementing positive change no matter the grunt work it took.

The relentlessness Edwin developed by consistently showing up day after day is the one commitment that took the seemingly impossible and made it possible. It is the same breakthrough service that cuts through every excuse for you and everyone around you. We are not the products of our surroundings, our upbringings, or any situation or circumstance that comes our way. We are the product of our consistency.

The simplest thing you can do is be relentlessly consistent. But it's also the most difficult thing you can do. If you can show up anywhere with relentless consistency, despite your fear of rejection, your background, or any other element, that is an act of breakthrough service that will reverberate into all your efforts.

Where do you allow rejection to deflect your breakthrough service?

***

The final buzzer had sounded almost three hours ago, but *everyone* was still celebrating in the locker room. It was a sensory smorgasbord of champagne, sweat, laughter, and the strobing flash of cameras. We all crowded near the NBA Trophy, deliriously excited to capture this moment as a permanent memory. We were here. The Toronto Raptors had just defeated the dynasty that was the Golden State Warriors on their home floor at Oracle Arena. I was overjoyed and bursting with pride, both for my uncle Nick, whose coaching had transformed the Raptors into champions, and for my friends on the team, Jeremy Lin, Norm Powell, and OG Anunoby.

I was taking a picture with Finals MVP Kawhi Leonard when I saw a man about my height push a stroller into the room, with his wife at his side. Anywhere else, it wouldn't have seemed unusual—a beautiful couple and their baby, out for a walk. In this room, at this moment, they certainly stood out. The man was dressed in full Golden State Warriors sweats.

It couldn't be who I thought it was. . . .

But my eyes weren't playing tricks on me. Steph Curry, Golden State Warriors' golden boy, one of the league's most dynamic players, best shooters, and just all-around highly respected superstars, was in the Raptors' locker room with his wife and kids.

He walked through the locker room, shaking the hand of each player, coach, front office member—and even the water boy. He genuinely congratulated them on their championship victory.

Steph Curry didn't immediately drag himself home after his team's dynasty came crumbling down. Instead he waited for three hours and gave the Raptors the opportunity to celebrate each other alone. Then he went out of his way to drop by and express his admiration by celebrating the accomplishments of "the enemy" after they not only defeated his team, but also stole his chance to be cemented as one of the greatest *ever* to play the game.

Unreal.

But that's who he was. Steph Curry was fun-loving, a great teammate, and an encouraging superstar. His reputation preceded him, yes—but no one, and I mean *no one*, does what Steph did that night in the locker room. To this day, it is one of the greatest moments of genuine respect I have ever seen in professional sports—or in anything professional for that matter.

Character is not who you are when others are watching and you *have* to turn it on. Character is who you are when the bright lights are off and no eyes are on you. It is an act of incredible breakthrough service to show up as your best self at all times—to celebrate victories regardless of whether they are your own. To celebrate others' victories even when they are at your expense.

It doesn't matter who you are or how much the world has told you that your time and attention are worth. You can be the same exact person on camera as you are off. You can act in breakthrough service by being relentlessly consistent and always being present. Being a BIOnic leader requires looking outside yourself and gaining the perspective of the world. If you want to serve your breakthrough and your team with genuine, effective leadership, you have to be able to serve that to everyone in every situation. Not just when it benefits you, not just when it is easy, and not just when you feel like it. You will stand next to other elite performers in every walk of life, and you must respect and celebrate the contribution of every single one. No matter your level of talent or stature, you will face moments of frustration, anger, disappointment, and hurt. Those are the most critical times to act in breakthrough service.

Where is it most uncomfortable for you to act charitably?

WHERE'S THE CONNECTION?

Making connections is a critical component of building your breakthrough cooperation, but it can also be an incredible act of breakthrough service. The twist is that you're not focused on building your own connections—you're connecting others, so that they have the opportunities to cultivate the relationships for their own breakthrough teams. Utilize the breakthrough cooperation skills you practice in your own life in service to others without any concern for what you are getting back.

Plus, it's easy. You know one person, and you know another person. The two of them don't know each other—that's a quick introductory email to send. Boom! Breakthrough service, right?

But it's not that simple. It is important when making connections (and in all acts of your breakthrough service) to act with thought and care. Good intentions are not enough. If you are not thinking about the people you are serving and how you can benefit them, you are acting more in service of yourself and your ego. Making connections for others can be an invaluable breakthrough service as long as you take the time to think and understand their missions, drives, and complements.

Unlike your own connections, you can't cultivate ones you make in service for others. That responsibility falls on them. But you do need to make sure that there's something substantial there to cultivate!

***

I swear, I thought he was a myth—no one seemed to actually know what "the man who knows everyone" even looked like. He was behind Allen Iverson, behind LeBron James, behind _____ (you can fill in the blank with any NBA player or even hip-hop mogul). Malice at the Palace? Yeah, he was there, and was the only man who could hold back a red-hot angry Ron Artest. Rumors about Wes abounded in whispers (most of which ended up being verified eventually). He roomed with Michael Jordan at basketball camp when they were kids. He rubbed shoulders with U.S. presidents. Phil Knight brought him in to consult on how to grow Nike. He created a mind-boggling $120 million dollar marketing deal for LeBron. He was everywhere. You were never more than a few conversations away from hearing about another mysterious connection he had or another industry-altering deal that he was putting together. "World Wide Wes" supposedly knew anyone you desperately wanted to know . . . but no one seemed to know him personally.

When GQ finally did an expose on this mystery man, people diligently read every line to try and figure him out, but the truth was stranger and simpler than fiction: he had his hand in every jar because *he wasn't taking from the jars*. As Reebok Executive Tom Shine said, "He's never asked me for anything. Wes doesn't have a hidden agenda."

There are very few people in the world like Wes who can give so freely without at least holding *something* back for themselves. People will do anything and everything to get close to this kind of person. And I was lucky to learn from the most mysterious master of breakthrough service ever to grace basketball— William Wesley, World Wide Wes himself.

It was one of my first visits to the big city of Los Angeles, and the bright lights scared me as much as they intrigued me. LA can be very overwhelming for a kid coming from the farmlands of the Midwest. They say everything is bigger in Texas; wait until you get to LA. As much as I wanted to turn and run in those early days, this was the mecca of basketball. If I wanted to make it in this industry, I had to learn the ropes, and fast.

Walking into the Hangar in Santa Monica alongside my friend and only NBA connection, Gary Sacks, was the most intimidating experience of my young life. The Hanger had been a small airport, renovated and transformed into a basketball arena; this weekend, it was host to the Nike All-American Basketball Camp. The top high school and college players were there to showcase their talent in front of a full house of NBA coaches and GMs. I was outclassed and outdone —every identity

I'd collected in my first twenty-some years, from top player to top coach to top networker meant nothing in this sea of talent. I was honored just to be in the room, breathing the same air.

I didn't want to be a nuisance to Gary, so I slipped away to find a seat in the bleachers by myself. There were still a few people around, but I was careful to put myself at a distance so that no one would feel obligated to talk to me. I was the least exciting person in the room that night—I didn't want any of these people, on their basketball-critical missions, to mistake me for someone they should waste their time and talent on.

"How's it going, kid? What's your story?"

I turned towards the man in the Nike tracksuit sitting at my ten o'clock and launched into the new spiel I'd been practicing: "I'm good. I'm David, I run basketball camps and do workouts for NBA players."

I paused, remembering where I was—just because I didn't recognize this guy didn't mean anything. He could have been the shadow king of the NBA, for all I knew. "Okay, that's a stretch—I've done one workout for *one* NBA player so far. But I'm working on more!"

The man turned his head and smiled at me. "That's great, that's what you love to do?"

"Yeah, I love it. I absolutely love it. I want to be an NBA coach someday; that's my goal."

No response.

I must have overstepped my boundaries. I knew I shouldn't tell people that; way too unrealistic. I was sure this man was just letting the comment slide instead of laughing in my face.

About thirty seconds went by before the man in the Nike jumpsuit said, "I want to introduce you to my friend Goro Nakajima."

"Okay," I managed to squeak out.

The man picked up his phone, and within minutes, I was shaking hands with Goro, the head of everything Nike Basketball International. He was the one who brought Yao Ming to the NBA from China, and the one who handled international relations for MJ, Kobe, all of the greats.

"David wants to work the Nike All-Asia Camp. Can you make this happen?" the man in the jumpsuit asked Goro.

I froze. I never said that. I didn't even know what the Nike All-Asia Camp was. Now, Goro, this man with immense power in the basketball world, was probably thinking I was asking for outlandish things.

I barely had time to start panicking before Goro responded, "Absolutely," and asked for my email and cell number.

The next day, I had an email offer for the Nike All-Asia Camp shooting coach position, which kicked everything off. I went to China and earned the respect of my coaching peers—and the friendship and trust of Goro, who would eventually recommend me as a shooting coach to the Brooklyn Nets years later. That short interaction on the bleachers of a renovated airport began my career in the NBA. The man in the Nike jumpsuit handed me the key to my breakthrough without asking for a thing. I never even asked his name. When Goro told me, years later, that I was yet another benefactor of the breakthrough service of World Wide Wes, I began to recognize how such a man could amass the power and the breakthrough cooperation of so many. If he ever came to me and told me to place my trust in someone else, no matter how unproven, I would give it in a heartbeat.

Just as being a cultivator is key to breakthrough cooperation, being a connector for others without focusing on what you could possibly gain from it, is an incredible act of breakthrough service. It's something great basketball players learn on the court from leaders like Erving "Magic" Johnson, who earned five NBA championship rings with the Showtime Los Angeles Lakers. Magic is such a legend, he almost doesn't seem real. Who could average *that* many points per game, win *that* many championships, and handle the ball *that* well? But Magic's greatest ability was the most mundane, the most ordinary. It's something no highlight reel captured, yet it was a critical moment preceding every memorable play. Magic Johnson *set up* assists. All point guards can pass and rack up assists, but Magic didn't just toss the ball to his teammate: he made sure his teammates were in their sweet spots, where they each would have the most potential to score. Trust me, there is a huge difference.

As a three-point shooter, I shine in a very specific, targeted pocket on the court; if a teammate passes me the ball when I'm in rhythm, stepping into my shot at the top of the key dead center, it's going in ten times out of ten. If a pass comes to my feet and I'm off-balance, who knows?

A teammate who concentrates on assists is often more valuable than any individual shooter; he plays a role in each and every shot any player on the team takes. And Magic concentrated on his setup assists time and time again. Throughout his NBA career, he *averaged* 11.19 assists per game, which was head and shoulders above the second-place holder, John Stockton.

From pickup games to NBA practices, ball hogs are terrible on the court. I don't care if you're one of the best shooters in the world—pass the ball. Yes, even to the player who doesn't shoot as well as you do. *Especially* to that guy! No one grows if they never shoot! Act in breakthrough service and set up awesome assists.

That goes double for the workplace. No matter how well-intentioned, the "Here, Just Let Me Do It" bosses destroy morale. They create an atmosphere where employees don't try to do their jobs as well as they can, much less improve. If it's not your job, stop hogging the ball. Be a BIOnic leader—take the time to set up your struggling subordinates with great assists, and they'll keep advancing.

But honestly, this failure of BIOnic leadership starts closer to home. At home, actually. Doing homework and school projects, and making calls to teachers or other parents to resolve your child's personal issues—is there anything you *won't* do for your kid?

Yes, you're way better and faster at building a baking soda volcano, but they need that long-term personal growth. Instead of doing the work for them, embrace the Magic Johnson within you and set your kids up for success. Show them how to do the project, then hand the reins over. Teach them how to make a call to an adult, then let them dial. Teach them how to use their words to stand up against bullies. Having difficult experiences isn't always the worst thing for them, but not having a backbone is.

Magic Johnson could have scored every basket, but that wouldn't have made any of his other teammates better. You can do everything for your kids, co-workers, and teammates, but that will never serve them in the long run. Be a BIOnic leader and make the connection assists for people so they can do it themselves. It's a much greater breakthrough service than just handing out solutions.

Where are you "hogging" rather than "assisting"?

***

When I turned thirty-one, the vision of my career path ahead started getting hazy. I'd been training NBA players for eight years, and I could definitely keep going, at least for a while. But it was starting to wear on my body, and my heart was getting restless. I could always pivot and focus more heavily on the health and wellness optimization I had integrated into my coaching over the past couple of years. But there was another (far foggier and less practical) path, too: motivational speaking and publishing the book I'd been writing in my spare time.

I knew that I wanted to be around elite minds and high achievers. I'd spent most of my career on the courts, so I didn't know nearly as many people in the health and leadership spaces. Basketball people connect by being in the same room—physically in the same arenas. Leaders in these other fields seemed to exist mostly online, and their status was projected in their follower counts. I didn't have a social media following; my Instagram likes hovered around between forty-five and fifty if I *really* had the filter and caption on point.

I figured if I could just get a few of these leaders in a room together for dinner, I could learn from them and develop relationships with them. If I really did it right and got the perfect match of leaders, I would be serving them greatly. As a bonus, they would always remember me as the one who put them together. But only if it was the right match.

It wouldn't be the first time I tried to be the Great Connector. Between Magic Johnson's assists on court and Wes's assists in real life, I understood this breakthrough service, and I had nothing but admiration and appreciation for it. When I'd tried to emulate these masters, though, I'd hit some snags. I tried to operate with the selflessness Wes had shown me, but throwing friends together to connect wasn't a breakthrough service.

There is a big difference between connecting mutual friends in the hopes they'll hit it off and doing some of the strategic, purposeful legwork to make sure they can work in breakthrough cooperation together.

I put in some real time scanning profiles trying to decide who to invite to a breakthrough dinner. I couldn't fill it with only my friends or just pick random people. And what if there were no shared interests? What if they didn't like each other?

The conversation would die, and I would be remembered as the host of this painful event.

I started playing with formulas to match people's missions, goals, and commonalities, in order to better sift through profiles and estimate the probability of a successful connection. The connection calculator was born, and very shortly, I knew exactly who I was going to invite to this dinner:

Max Lugavere, NYT best-selling nutrition expert

Lewis Howes, NYT best-selling lifestyle entrepreneur and an iTunes Top 100 podcast host

Mark Sisson, NYT best-selling nutrition author and the top health and wellness guy for many years

Khalil Rafati, founder/owner of Malibu Beach Yoga and SunLife Organics, author and speaker

Khalil, the only one I vaguely knew, offered to hook this dinner up at the exclusive Soho House in Malibu.

I slipped into the DMs of the other three on my list to invite them to the dinner and tell them a little about myself. I was shocked when they all confirmed they would be there and expressed how excited they were to meet each other.

All five of us got together and had an epic three-hour dinner: laughter, great conversations, and vulnerability I never thought would be shared over a first meeting. I didn't say much (I didn't really know what to say), but I listened, asked questions, and made sure everyone was having a good time.

They did, and that dinner cemented our friendship. More importantly, it led to a web of breakthrough cooperation and breakthrough service. These guys appeared on each other's podcasts and started cross-promoting, which allowed them to reach each other's sizable markets. The connection calculator was a success; I'd acted in breakthrough service.

I have put on nearly twenty of these high-level dinners since, facilitating great connections that have changed the lives and elevated the missions of very high-level individuals. All because I realized the breakthrough service I could provide with the connection calculator, the ultimate assist machine. I didn't just pass the ball; I went straight Magic Johnson mode and set everyone up for their highest level of success. That's what being a true connector is all about.

We all have "shooting pockets," our sweet spots where we're perfectly positioned to receive the ball. As leaders, through years of studying the people we interact with, leaning on our gut intuition, and actively asking how we can best set people up, we learn where their "shooting pockets" are.

A BIOnic leader can tell where people are strong, where they need help, and what roadblocks are keeping them from becoming the best versions of themselves. Instead of cookie-cutter leading, we are able to find each person's shooting pockets, setting them up for instant success and long-term growth.

Where are your connections' shooting pockets?

***

BREAKTHROUGH SERVICE KEYS

- We need multiple perspectives of the world to understand any situation.

- Challenge and support.

- Be curious, ask questions. Listening isn't a passive activity.

- To become *outstanding*, we must go through a period of obsession.

- Keep showing up everywhere to act with charity and respect.

- Character is who you are when the cameras are off.

- Connect with purpose, not with concern for personal gain.

- Set up assists.

BREAKTHROUGH SERVICE TOOL: CONNECTION CALCULATOR

Breakthrough service means always being on the lookout for unrecognized needs. Challenge yourself to identify at least two elite performers you can help connect to complement their own breakthroughs. These connections can be professional or personal—the only requirement is choosing the most thoughtful, strategic connection possible.

Enter the Connection Calculator!

There are five factors that I weigh and consider when I'm making connections for others:

1. Reflective Missions: Are these people on similar or complementary missions? (A baker and an auto mechanic might not be the right match.).

2. Complementary Passion Projects: How do they express their missions —do they have podcasts? Did they write books? Do they work in similar mediums?

3. Distance on the Path: Have these people grown their missions to similar points? (It might not serve both parties well to connect someone with 500 Instagram followers to someone with 500,000, depending on the other factors.)

4. Rise Factor: Would this meeting be a needle mover in their lives?

5. Serving Hearts: If the opportunity arose, would each person help the other?

If you can't mark off at least four of these, you should consider recalibrating. If you can hit four out of five funneling factors, you have a match. And if you hit five out of five, you have a home run!

CHAPTER 6

Q4: Tasting Why:
Breakthrough Purpose

Once you know yourself and your team, and you are serving the world around you, your breakthroughs are so close that you can almost taste them. We've covered the who, what, and where, but the "why"—*why are you playing?*—is a deeply personal question. The answer determines how meaningful and fulfilling your breakthrough life will be. In the words of Viktor Frankl, "He who knows the 'why' for his existence . . . will be able to bear almost any 'how.'"

Your breakthrough purpose is why you exist. It determines what you pursue with relentless consistency at all times. It's what you're driven to pursue even after a day full of disappointments, disagreements, or miscommunications. It is not what you're "sometimes interested" in doing; it is what you have to pursue all the time, in order to feel the most whole. Exploring your confidence, cooperation, and service will lead you to your purpose. What you need to develop now is "relentless consistency."

Are you someone whom others would automatically characterize as being consistent? Are you consistent in who you are, and in what you stand for? Can others rely on you consistently? Or are you like a chameleon, constantly changing with your surroundings and reacting to whatever the world throws at you like it is bigger than the breakthrough you want to achieve?

The most important player you can be in the NBA, the real gold standard, is the "clutch player." That's the player who is still focused, still physically, mentally, and emotionally there in the final quarter, win or lose. He's the player who everyone else on the court draws their strength from, who remembers his bigger purpose all the way through, who recognizes the team can still have a breakthrough, who inspires other teammates' breakthroughs, and who can make those breakthroughs actually happen.

Being *relentlessly consistent* is the single greatest determining factor for breakthrough results. It is the culmination of your confidence, of the strength of your team, and of the impact you have on others. It's the difference between lucky inspiration and living a breakthrough life.

WHY DRIVE?

We are all driven, all motivated by some internal fire. But not everyone has notable amounts of *drive* (though, I will say, it is much more prevalent in elite performers). "Drive" is a word that gets thrown around as much as *culture, mindset, grit,* and any other extremely broad, abstract term. And don't confuse ambition for *drive*. Ambition is wanting to reach a destination. Drive is the part of you that can't rest until you get there. In the NBA world, I'm looking for the answer to "Do you drag me to the gym, or do I have to drag you?" Does the player really want it? Is he willing to put in the unseen hours, the 6 a.m. workouts, and the long off-season summer days? Or is he just in it for the lifestyle and the glitz and glamour? I can tell you within ten minutes of meeting a player whether he has this golden goose gift of *drive*.

But there are some—a very, very select few—whose drive is so intense, it is synonymous with their breakthrough purpose.

***

Shai Gilgeous-Alexander had it. All the scouts knew it. This gangly nineteen-year-old kid who was fresh off his only season playing basketball at the University of Kentucky was destined to be a first-round draft pick based solely on his height, length, and potential upside.

But before I can train shooters to get better, I have to determine where they are weak. With some people, that's easy. Young kids with crazy talent and drive, though? That's more difficult. They have the adrenaline, the energy, and the sheer stamina to motor through a lot. I have to wear them down so I can see what mistakes they start making when they get tired, and if they get bored at any point. Energy ebbs and flows, but the greatest shooters can remain laser-focused with perfect mechanics while dealing with a hurricane of off-court problems. I've put a lot of effort into constructing a workout that could wear down even a racehorse, and Shai was going to get this full treatment.

He showed up early for our first morning of training. He walked into the Santa Monica gym, threw on his shoes, and immediately started shooting. And shooting, and shooting, and shooting. No warm-up, and never slowing down. No matter how hard I made it, Shai kept asking for more and more.

After nearly three hours, my hungry stomach began eating itself, so I declared our first session done. Complete. There was nothing more that could be accomplished today.

Shai nodded, then said, "What time do you want to go tonight?"

What?!

His performance in our first session was impressive, but what Shai showed me in that moment (and proved over and over afterwards), was that he had a special quality that scouts weren't privy to knowing. Shai *lived* for the unseen hours. He embraced being in the gym alone with no one was watching. Now, don't get me wrong—Shai *loves* competing in the bright lights. But he's not driven just by his performance, or the fame, or any accolades the NBA could hand out. Shai is driven to see how far he can stretch his elite strength. Shai's driven to find his personal best.

Knowing in a heartbeat that this kid was going to take years off my life, I told him to meet me that evening at UCLA.

Our evening workout was just as intense as the one we had that morning. We snuck into a recreational student gym so we could get up as many shots as we wanted. Well, as many shots as I wanted, and then a few hundred more. There weren't enough shots on the planet to fulfill Shai's desire.

When I declared once again that our session would have to be over, Shai made a fatal error. He challenged me to a three-point shootout.

Three-point shooting is my specialty. I'll often showcase it immediately to put young NBA talents in their place; it's my way of showing them that it doesn't matter who else has let them believe they are the GOAT, they still will benefit by listening to me because I can torch them in a shootout. As expected, I won the shootout with Shai in a landslide.

"Let's go grab some dinner," I said as I strutted to the sidelines, feeling good about myself. I assumed the next words out of his mouth would be "Yeah, I'm starving."

Instead, I got "I need a rematch."

Not what I expected. Certainly not what I wanted. I had been on the court with Shai for over five hours, and it was only our first day. My body needed nourishment and rest!

Reluctantly, I played him. And handily beat him again.

"Run it back," Shai said immediately, a look of killer determination on his face. "I ain't leaving until I beat you."

"Alright," I said. "But I already warned you, you aren't going to beat me."

And just like that, Shai transformed from a gangly, goofy, smiley teen to a man on a mission. He vibrated with laser focus.

Shai didn't miss. Not one. He made all twenty-five three-point shots, beating me by four total. He didn't say a word after; he just looked at me, smiled, and winked.

I was speechless: how had he just done that? He hadn't made more than sixteen the two previous times, yet now he somehow made all twenty-five. It was simple: it was his purpose. Shai refused to lose, and there was no chance he was leaving that gym without a victory. So, he willed himself to another level.

Shai Gilgeous-Alexander wasn't cut from the same cloth as most people. He wasn't even made of the same stuff as other NBA players. That day, I knew right then and there, that Shai was destined for greatness in the NBA. He would become an elite, franchise-changing player. It was his breakthrough purpose.

Three years into his career, Shai is now one of the top point guards in the league. He doesn't just have potential, he has a purpose. He was, is, and always will be made for this purpose.

Shai had *it*, the definition of *drive*. And like Shai, you will know you've found your breakthrough purpose when you are driven to do it in the off-hours, driven to make sure that you never lose any ground, and driven to will yourself to the next level. It is what you do when the lights are out and no one is watching, in the *unseen* hours. To find your breakthrough purpose, you just have to ask yourself what you are driven to do, obsessed with doing, when no one is watching. Even when the victory seems impossible. When you are out of options and out of energy, what still spurs you to stand up tall and make the impossible real?

Besides Shai, I've only heard of two other NBA players who had the type of obsessive drive that signals they have found their breakthrough purpose in basketball. One is Michael Jordan; the myth and legend of his obsessive drive are so huge, it's sometimes hard to separate fact from fiction. The other player, I learned about from Ed Schilling, who is my good friend, mentor, and personal definition of relentless consistency.

In 1996, Ed was an assistant coach for the New Jersey Nets, and in charge of running the predraft workouts. (Funny how life works: exactly twenty years later, I was doing the same exact thing for the newly named Brooklyn Nets.)

NBA predraft workouts are brutal—think Navy SEALS "hell week," but for basketball. They are designed to break young players and test them on their ability to play through fatigue. Predraft workouts can be the most grueling month of an NBA player's entire career: red-eye flights traveling from coast to coast; back-to-back-to-back days of early morning workouts, conditioning tests, and going up against other talented players trying to come for your throat; and extensive personality testing by the team's psychiatrists.

Ed was running an excruciating workout that extended well past two hours. Players had their hands on their knees, gasping for air; they were physically and mentally drained. As soon as they heard the final buzzer signal that the workout was complete, the players immediately hightailed it to the locker room where they could sprawl out on the floor. Only one player stayed behind, a young, talented seventeen-year-old kid. The youngest player in the 1996 NBA draft. He was relatively unknown, but had promising ability.

He bounded up to Ed after the workout and said, "That was great! Thank you for showing me all those drills." He then gushed about a drill Ed ran that he had never seen before, and how much it could help his game. In the NBA, it was a basic, mundane footwork drill. But the kid wanted it and he ate it up. Two more hours went by as the young player practiced only that footwork, asking Ed for incremental improvements, even though most would have called his mechanics already flawless. Finally, he had it mastered, hours after the rest of the players had hit the locker room.

Ed was stunned, blown away by this kid's commitment to self-mastery. He knew he was in the presence of someone special—someone whose breakthrough purpose was basketball.

This kid, Kobe Bryant, did not disappoint.

Why is it that you are driven to push yourself beyond all human limits and possibilities?

Why Process?

Everything is a system. Systems use processes; processes produce results.

$$\text{System} + \text{Process} = \text{Results}$$

You have your breakthrough system—the confidence, cooperation, service, and purpose. You have the process to work through the system—answering the who, what, where, and why. Answer your why by falling in love with the process, and you'll live a life full of daily breakthroughs.

When you live for the process, when you define your success more by how you are playing rather than by the final score, you have found a breakthrough purpose. Be confident enough to measure your own worth by the work you are doing; don't fall for the trap of insecurely compiling your stats for other people to judge.

It sounds so basic, something we teach a child—yet we still somehow define our value in our stat sheets at the expense of our real work, joy, and purpose—the process. If you're drawn to questions like, "How can we become the top player in our industry?" or "How do I become MVP?" then you need to pivot your focus to your fundamentals. Putting the worth of your breakthrough into the hands of other people creates a hole within you that can never be filled. Live for the process, and you'll create results naturally and joyfully.

***

Norm Powell: the 46th pick in the 2013 NBA draft.

How many second-round draft picks last in the NBA? Less than 5 percent.

Norm wasn't fazed; he had overcome the odds his entire life. Growing up in poverty, Norm had to fight tooth and nail for everything he got. He wasn't heavily recruited out of high school, but UCLA threw him a last-minute offer after they swung and missed on their five top recruits.

Norm didn't play much his freshman year, but saw more time as a sophomore, and flourished in his junior year. It was time to prove that he had what it took to achieve the only dream he ever had. He officially entered the NBA draft.

On June 25, 2015, Norm's dream came true, but what he thought would be a breakthrough night unfortunately turned bitter. He was supposed to be a late first-round draft pick; first rounders are given signing bonuses and guaranteed three-year contracts. Second-round draft picks are given . . . nothing. Absolutely nothing. Not only was Norm drafted dead smack in the middle of the second round, he was also traded immediately by the Milwaukee Bucks and sent to the Toronto Raptors.

Norm worked his butt off to make the Raptors team, and he secured a rookie scale contract of less than $500,000 (which might seem like a lot, but in the NBA world, it's not much). Of the fifteen players who were selected between pick 45 and 60 of that 2013 draft, Norm was one of just three ever to play in an

NBA game, so that alone was a victory. He even started in the playoffs, matched up against the great Dwayne Wade. But he couldn't crack the rotation, and was rarely given the opportunity to play consistent minutes. When he did get in the game, if he missed a shot, he was yanked out at the next dead ball. It ate at Norm; he was stuck in a *results* mindset, judging his success based solely on his box score numbers. Norm's mood and self-worth fluctuated from game to game.

Norm's sixth year in the NBA was make-or-break. He would either be defined as a career substitute who could give a team a spark from time to time, or he would break through and become a star.

Eight years prior, when I was just some random kid putting on workouts for whomever wanted them, Norm showed up at the gym and busted his butt for me. At the time he was just about to start his sophomore season at UCLA. After years of working together, Norm trusted me; the bond we developed had become unbreakable. I knew we had to change something in Norm's mindset to make him the player he was meant to be. What if, instead of basing his self-worth and self-confidence on the points per game and field goal percentage stats, he based it on the *process?*

Norm's best two moves were catch-and-shoot threes and attacking the hoop in transition. I suggested that we only track how many times he was able to correctly position himself for the shot, instead of how many buckets he actually made. I told him to focus only on the process, not the results.

This worked for a few games, but soon Norm forgot what he was focusing on. It was too hard in the heat of the battle to concentrate solely on the setup. He'd been focusing on seeing the ball go through the net his entire life.

I had seen the movie *Inception* and was fascinated by the way the spinning top was used as a trigger. Could this movie magic work for Norm? The next night, I challenged Norm to use the cue word "process" as many times as possible. It would be the word that triggered his subconscious to bring him back into focus. After his best personal game of the season, Norm reported back to me that during it he said "process" aloud 142 times. It had actually worked.

When the season was cut short due to the pandemic, Norm had just been named the Eastern Conference Player of the Week. The Western Conference Player of the Week? LeBron James.

When we hear about breakthroughs, we concentrate on the hero, the person who runs the final mile in a relay, the person who has the eureka moment of discovery, or the person who makes the basket right at the final buzzer. We concentrate on the results.

However, that hero moment in our favorite breakthrough stories is only a snapshot—a very misleading snapshot. We don't talk about how the vast majority of the breakthrough is spent in the process. Before that snapshot of the results, our is hero was developing their elite strengths, gathering their team and resources, gaining perspective, trying other possibilities—basically working their butt off. Find your breakthrough purpose by falling in love with the process, and the results will slip right into place. You'll be able to experience hero moment after hero moment, give a fist pump, and then dive back into your true breakthrough purpose—the process.

Why are you excited to do the work?

***

Fundamentals. I know, I know—blech. Who is going to choose broccoli when there's cake on the table? Heck, why do we even have to bother with the cake when we can just go straight for the frosting? How can our breakthrough purpose rely more on boring fundamentals than on something innovative and sexy? How can we possibly come up with something the world has never seen before if we're only focusing on the things people nail as the very first step?

In one of my favorite Bible verses, Luke 20:17, Jesus tells his followers, "The stone the builders rejected has become the cornerstone." How can the "rejected" stone become so critical? The fundamentals are the building blocks, the foundations, the rejected cornerstones that define the breakthrough we wish to achieve.

I got the opportunity to spend time with the Golden State Warriors during their preseason and the start of the 2015–2016 NBA season. The Warriors were fresh off winning the Championship; they were the elite of the elite, and had led the league in scoring, three-point shooting, and every stat that makes basketball flashy and beautiful. They were setting records and changing how the game was played offensively. I cried multiple times during the NBA Finals watching their majestic performance. So here I was, thinking, "Yes, this is my lucky break! I'm going to learn all of these in-depth secrets, tricks, the plays that make the Warriors great. I'm going to be able to steal this and use it in my own coaching, and before you know it, I'll be just like the Warriors—the greatest!"

A few weeks of practice went by, and I was still waiting to see all of this incredible magic up close. Instead, what I was seeing every single day, for at least an hour at the start of practice, was form shooting, dribbling, passing, and footwork. The basics. The boring basics. The most revolutionary NBA team in the past fifty years was working on the fundamentals relentlessly. I couldn't believe it. This was what made them so great? How the heck were some of the top players in the NBA buying into this BS? If I ran a middle school basketball camp without more dazzle, I would have an undersized mutiny on my boards!

There was a very large banner on the wall of the Warriors' gym that simply read "Joy." This was a reminder to every player and coach when they walked onto the floor that they were going to approach every practice with joy, with gratitude for being able to play this game they loved, and with relish for focusing on the fundamentals.

I was blown away. I couldn't believe it. I had expected a Barnum & Bailey Circus–level show, but there was nothing glitzy and glamorous about them. They were all about the daily persistence of being great in the fundamentals. And doing so with joy.

How did the Golden State Warriors do that season, you ask?

Best. Record. In. NBA. History.

We live in a world that celebrates the end product—the winning play, the beautiful Rembrandt that sells for millions, the perfectly plated dinner. We celebrate what we see, we celebrate the finishing stones. We don't see the thousands upon thousands of repetitive drills, of side-to-side brushstrokes, or of burned and mutilated dishes in the rearview. We cannot see that the stone that is rejected is actually what holds the whole structure together and makes it what it is. The only way to achieve greatness and find our breakthrough purpose is to stop looking at the end result and start focusing on the fundamentals.

The Golden State Warriors built their entire team culture on the process, and not even just the process but joyfully finding their breakthrough purpose in the absolute most basic components of the process. And after their championship hero moment, they fist-pumped—and then they went straight back to the gym the next day to resume working on the process.

You can find your breakthrough purpose in the process alone, like Norm. You can find it as a team, a company, a corporate culture. Let the rest of your industry live in the stats that drive them nuts, the ones they're trying to use to prove they're big dogs. That's the path to permanent insecurity—even when they stumble across a breakthrough hero moment, it will taste chalky and bland. Get so excellent at the fundamentals, that you'll actually find ways to make them even better. When you are secure and devoted to yourself, your relationships, and your service to the world, it naturally changes the way in which you think and operate. You have to learn the rules so well that you can break them. Those are the breakthroughs that blow the entire world away.

Why are you focused on your fundamentals?

WHY COMMIT?

Are you interested in your breakthrough, or are you committed?

There is a big difference between the two. If you're interested, you will do it when it feels right, when it's something you want to do. But when the going is tough and there's something more attractive drawing your attention, you won't.

But committed, that's an entirely different mindset. If you are committed to your values, they don't bend when someone more powerful suggests it. If you're committed to your process, there are no cheat days. If you're committed to your spouse, being unfaithful isn't even an option. Committed is recognizing there's no short-term diversions that are worth trading away even a second of the life you want. Strongly interested can look like committed—but that door is always left open at least a crack, and it will blow wide open one day.

Find your breakthrough purpose in commitment. When you commit, your breakthrough, your culture, and your values are your purpose. If you don't commit, they're just a costume.

***

I'm an early morning person, but 4 a.m. is a bit of a stretch. I was up before the sun for one reason and one reason alone: I was hunting the most dangerous game.

I hopped on the train holding a photo of my target. He was very short, bald, wore glasses, and hunched over. I power walked through the crowds (it is *always* crowded on the Tokyo trains), and through the back alleys until I reached my destination: the legendary Tisjuiki Market.

The intense smell engulfed my nostrils and stuck to my clothes for weeks after (just ask Taylor). I walked around, glancing at the fish, listening to the auctioneers raise bids on the prized tunas in rapid-fire Japanese—tunas that sold for upwards of $3,000 depending on size and quality.

I strolled through row after row of fish after fish after octopus after *I'm pretty sure that fish is dead but I'm not quite sure*, but nothing stood out to me. I scoured each stand looking for my target.

Hours went by; the sun was now rising over the ocean on the busy seaport. Tired, dejected, and about to pass out from the smell, I figured it was time to pack it in and call it a day. "He doesn't exist," I muttered to myself as I gave the market one last scan.

Someone caught my eye. My heart skipped three beats.

"Could that be him? Could that really be . . . Jiro?"

I had no other choice, I had to find out. This was my target, my entire reason for the journey. From the moment I saw the documentary *Jiro Dreams of Sushi*, I was determined to find the iconic sushi master. Not behind the counter of his Michelin three-star restaurant, but here, doing what he does, unaware he's even being observed.

I kept my distance, watching Jiro's every movement. He would pick up a fish, inspect it, smell it, feel the scales and the texture, even put his ear to it, like he was listening for the ocean through a seashell. And then, instead of purchasing it, he would put it down and move onto the next stand. A stand that had the same exact fish.

For an hour, Jiro performed the same routine at stall after endless stall—pick up the fish, inspect it all over, give it a big whiff, listen to it, and put it back down again and move on. I was hungry enough to eat one of those raw fish staring at me with their lifeless eyes, but I couldn't leave until I saw what made the difference—which fish Jiro would choose.

Finally, it happened. Jiro put the fish down on the counter, a bright red number that looked like a mix of a grouper and a tuna and something else that probably only swims in the waters of Japan. That was the one. That was the fish Jiro spent hours looking for. That was the fish he would serve that night.

Instead of going up to say something to him in my extremely broken and limited Japanese, I just stood back and soaked in what had just taken place.

It was artistry at its highest level. It was a sunrise over the Rocky Mountains, illuminating the sky with those perfect oranges, yellows, and pinks to which no picture can do justice. This was one of those moments I just had to sit back and enjoy for what it was.

Let's be honest—Jiro doesn't have to pay that much attention to the fish anymore. He's already built his reputation, he's already got the three stars, the documentary, and the cult following. Heck, he could probably have bulk orders of frozen mystery fish flown in from wherever and just pawn them off like the results of his painstaking efforts.

We see it all the time. The restaurant whose quality dips precipitously after building a fanatical following. The author who phones in the sequel to an amazing book. The movie franchise that started going stale after the third one, but somehow there are eighteen terrible, blockbuster follow-ups. The market builds a bubble that can sustain your mediocre next efforts.

However, bubbles burst and that's just a terrible, empty way to live. Something like 85 percent of people hate their jobs—they're only interested, not committed. When you're committed, you give everything you have, even if you might not actually enjoy the daily actions. Your breakthrough purpose echoes and reverberates off the most mundane details and gives them meaning.

BIOnic leaders don't "go through the motions." Even if you don't love every single detail, you are committed. Those motions have purpose. They become part of your bigger dream, your bigger breakthrough. Be Jiro and smell every fish that comes your way. He knows what it takes to be the best, and he won't settle for anything less. We weren't made to be average, we weren't made to be good, shoot we weren't even made to be great. We were made to be *outstanding!*

Why do you commit?

***

"We're Not for Everyone." And trust me, they make that abundantly clear. It hangs on a banner in their practice facility, it graces the walls of their locker room, it even is spelled out on the electronic signs at American Airlines Arena for their fans to see. This is the *Miami Heat Way*.

No one comes into Miami crooning Frank Sinatra's "I Did It My Way." That idea is squashed the moment a player signs on the dotted line to become part of the Heat. The Heat culture doesn't bend for anyone, not even the mighty LeBron James.

Erik Spoelstra is a very good friend of mine, part mentor, part brother. We love to nerd out about optimization, leadership, and everything personal development under the sun. Erik is the epitome of a *constant learner*—and that's where our similarities end. I love to talk, to interview people, and to be on podcasts. I even love being in front of a camera with a mic in my hand. Erik gets anxiety about speaking in public; he's an introvert to the core. It's interesting that one of the most successful coaches in NBA history doesn't like to speak in front of people—it seems like it would be a prerequisite. But that's where the beauty is found. Maybe that's why Erik has been so successful. Maybe that's why Erik was the only coach ever able to tame the lion that is LeBron James—not only one of the greatest players of all time, but also the greatest at getting coaches fired. Just ask David Blatt, Mike Brown, and a handful of others.

LeBron dropped his infamous "I'm taking my talents to South Beach" hammer on the city of Cleveland (his former team, where he was the "chosen one") on ESPN. He then went on to promise not one, not two, not three (and on and on until "not seven") championships. The rowdy South Beach crowd erupted with even more energy than they showed on New Year's Eve. LeBron didn't know what he was in for. But Erik did.

How do you get the player who *is* the franchise everywhere he goes to buy into the Miami Heat Way? A culture so strict with their players' bodies that they must pass a ridiculous series of conditioning drills that would challenge ultramarathoners? A team that measures body fat—not once or twice a year, like most teams, but once or twice per week. How do you get a guy who has had yes-men hanging around his entire life to sign up for that?

To start, Erik didn't dig his own grave by repeating the phrase every coach before him cursed themselves with: "LeBron, this is your team, I want you to lead the way you lead." That wasn't a Miami option. Sure, LeBron would be a leader of the team on the court, but leadership isn't about one person imposing beliefs, habits, and routines on everyone around them. It's about molding all the personalities and talents together for the mission.

Erik earned the nickname "No Problem" in 1995, the year he started with the Miami Heat. They needed someone to make a sandwich run—"No problem." They needed someone to go pick up laundry—"No problem." They needed someone to stay late tonight and tomorrow night and every night to put together film clips for the upcoming opponents—"No problem." Any menial task, they knew to ask Erik. His commitment to his team, his organization, his culture, was unwavering. Every day.

Erik was tasked with developing a video department where they could break down film of their games and upcoming opponents; something that had never previously existed in the NBA. (And something that seems so mainstream today, it's almost laughable it wasn't around back then.) He knew nothing about breaking down film, editing it, or even the coordination of editing. No problem. He committed to pouring his very best into the development of the NBA film room.

Spoelstra was the Miami Heat's dungeon master for four years. That's what they called it, "the dungeon." No windows, one door, a closet/casket with mounds of VHS. Spoelstra embraced the dungeon. He was committed to the Miami Heat. Not interested—committed.

In 1999, Erik was promoted to advanced scout. In 2008, thirteen years after "No Problem" walked through the front doors and into the dungeon, Erik Spoelstra was made the head coach of the Miami Heat. No one does that. That's the level of commitment Erik had—he made the impossible happen because he was that committed to the Heat's culture. There was no

singular player on Earth who could sway Erik from his commitment. He didn't forget where he had come from.

Erik doesn't talk much about the confrontations, arguments,
and struggles with coaching LeBron. That's not what the Heat
culture is about. They function as one; they move as a pack. If
you throw one person under the bus, you throw them all. They
don't work on "finding themselves," they work on "empowering
their team."

Miami did it, to the tune of two championships. Not quite
the seven LeBron promised, but bringing the Heat to the top of
the NBA and solidifying it as a place every player in the NBA
wanted to go was a feat in itself. A culture that was once feared by
free agents throughout the league as solitary confinement became
the highest sought destination, even by the greatest individual
players. They saw LeBron flourish into the player he was destined
to be—not by doing it all by himself, but by doing it all with others.

Erik Spoelstra didn't tell the players how to do it; he led
them. He created one of the most elite cultures in all of sports
because he was already entirely committed to it. Not interested,
not open to bending for a superstar. Committed. His breakthrough purpose was his commitment to the team, not to one
individual player or to one championship.

Commit to your breakthrough. Commit to the best for and
from your entire team, not one player. If your values shift to suit
one person, if they change with every market fluctuation and
opportunity, they aren't cooperative values anyone can rely on.
Build a culture of leaders committed to your breakthrough, and
don't even flirt with throwing that away to get one person interested. Find your breakthrough purpose in the strength to commit, and you will break through—exactly the way you dream.
No compromise.

Why is your breakthrough bigger than any one person?

WHY LOVE?

Your breakthrough might not belong to you.

We have our missions and dreams. But so do our families, our co-workers, our students, anyone we'll ever interact with, and even those we'll never meet. We can commit to our achievements, but we might find our greatest breakthroughs when the ones we love win.

Do you know who you love? Is it just a few? Is it many? Love is a service, a sacrifice, and a breakthrough purpose that resonates with very few. If you have the strength to set your breakthrough purpose in loving others, and you have the fortitude to prioritize helping the ones you love break through, you will never see every result. Because your breakthrough will never end.

***

Before Cori Close was *Cori Close*, one of the top women's college basketball coaches (coaching Team USA Women's Basketball speaks for itself!), she was a frustrated young UCLA assistant coach in search of a breakthrough. She knew her mission, and it was a simple enough combination: she wanted to be a championship-level coach, and she wanted to positively impact her players' lives. Unfortunately, the vast majority of coaches will tell you to choose: it's one or the other. This ate at Cori, to the point where she questioned whether coaching was truly her calling.

Despite Cori's struggles, Steve Lavin (the very successful UCLA men's head coach) saw something in her that stood out. As Cori rolled off the court one evening after an intense practice, Steve asked if she wanted to join him and a couple of other coaches for a special dinner. Cori asked if she had time to clean up and change first, but Steve told her it was now or never.

Glancing between Steve, who was known for his heavily gelled hair and *GQ* style, and her own sweaty joggers, Cori only hesitated for a second. If her friends and colleagues could handle it, she could too.

What Steve had neglected to mention was that the dinner was at the home of John Wooden—the famous and beloved UCLA coach who had won seven NCAA Championships in a row, and was one of the most quoted and inspirational humans of all time. The Wooden Triangle, Wooden-isms—his list of *drop the mic* quotes could fill every page of this book. Cori had studied him, idolized him, and wanted to be the female version of him. If there was anyone who could teach her about coaching winning teams while positively impacting the players' lives, it was John Wooden—of course she was in sweats!

Coach Wooden immediately looked at Cori and asked her name.

"Cori," she managed to mumble out.

"How do you spell that?"

"C-O-R-I," she responded.

The greatest coach in men's college basketball history lit up. "I want to show you something."

He led Cori out to his garden and pointed at a bench. The golden engraved plaque at the top of the bench read "Cori."

"You are the only one I've ever heard spell their name exactly like my great-granddaughter, so I know you are destined for greatness. You are going to lead so many young women and have an immense impact in their lives," Coach Wooden said, with a larger-than-life smile across his face.

John Wooden cares about me, Cori thought. *Here I am, just an assistant coach, and the great John Wooden not only took the time to talk to me, but he took the time to pour into me.*

Although it sounds like a small thing, John Wooden could read Cori and see that the most helpful thing for her was a small, highly personal connection. He was able to lead her by instantly treating her like family, and giving her the strength, despite her nervousness, to ask him for the guidance and support a family member would give.

Could my idol actually become my mentor? Cori wondered.

And that he did.

Cori started visiting him regularly, and John taught her how to effectively use his family style of leadership to win on the court *and* empower her players to win at life. Cori and John Wooden got together at his house every Tuesday for fifteen years; even when Cori took the head coaching job at Santa Barbara, she drove down to spend her Tuesdays with Coach Wooden.

Everyone knows about the impact John Wooden had on his teams and the people he took under his wing. Everyone knows that he shared his breakthrough purpose with so many by creating a family around him everywhere he went. What people don't realize is the sacrifice his flesh-and-blood family had to make. Sure, John loved his family and spent a lot of time with them, but being a mentor to others and pouring so much into people like Cori took time. His family had to accept that they weren't always going to get John; others needed him. His impact was immense, and even when his family didn't want to share his time with others, they knew it was their duty. It was their calling. It was their legacy to share John's legacy.

Coach Wooden passed away in 2010, but his legacy will never die. Cori became the UCLA head coach in 2011, and she is known throughout the basketball community for carrying his torch of creating winning teams *and* making a positive impact on players' lives. I am personally a legacy beneficiary of John Wooden's generosity of spirit and breakthrough purpose. Cori took me under her wing when I was finding my way in Los Angeles, and not only gave me a coaching consulting job with her UCLA Bruins Women's team, but allowed me to live rent-free in one of her guest rooms while I found my footing.

And that's where we can taste our breakthrough purpose, when we realize that our impact on one person can have a rippling impact on so many others. Like the acorns of a mighty oak tree can be carried anywhere in the world, we have amazing gifts to share that will reach other people we will never even meet. Our breakthroughs will help them grow, even if we never know about it. Don't consider the size of your breakthrough impact on people when you're building your breakthrough purpose; it's something you will never know. Trust me, if you treat every interaction like it has intentional, empowering impact, it will.

Why not create a legacy of leaders?

***

You may find your breakthrough purpose in the service and cooperation you give to many. You may also find it in just one. Your breakthrough purpose can be your greatest partnership with your ultimate co-conspirator and collaborator, the person you play the game with best, the person who drives you and your breakthrough beyond where you could ever take it alone.

Jordan and Kobe were two of the greatest, most individually offensively skilled players ever to set foot on a basketball court. Watching tapes of these men is like hearing the top violinist in the world pull notes from the heavens. It's poetry in motion.

But not alone. Never alone.

Without Pippen, Jordan never won a playoff series or a championship. Not one.

Kobe Bryant needed Shaq. Desperately. Together, Kobe and Shaq won three NBA Championships from 2000 to 2002; the year Kobe pushed Shaq out of town to prove he could do it alone, he didn't come close to sniffing the Finals. It took Kobe seven years to assemble a squad that could boost him back to the level he had played in cooperation with Shaq. By the time he won his next title, Kobe was already on the back end of his career.

Jordan and Kobe are all-time greats, two of the best *ever* to play the game. There is no debating that. But without their partners in crime, would they have been able to accomplish what they did? No chance. Certain people's chemistries only operate on a higher plane when they are in contact. Their breakthrough purpose is to boost each other and play the game together.

There is a moment in our lives when we realize this final quadrant of the breakthrough formula in all its beauty. There is a moment when it just *clicks*. The happy accident becomes a rhythm, a song in our head, a taste on our tongues, illuminating the light within us to everyone else.

I realized the power of my breakthrough purpose at one specific instant, as the doors swung open on the rooftop of the Marina del Rey Marriott. My mentor, Ed Schilling, was at my side, and my ten best friends—my team, my supporters and my challengers, my iron sharpens iron—stood behind me. Walking down the aisle was the most beautiful woman I had ever laid eyes on; in twelve minutes, she would be my wife.

Taylor walked up to the altar, and my thirty-one years of life flashed before my eyes. Everything I had done up until that point, I had been living for myself. It was all about me. In that moment, it all shifted: "I will serve my wife before my own needs." (Exact vows—Taylor will happily confirm.)

As a person who was convinced the world revolved around me for a good portion of my life, it felt *wonderful* to know it didn't. It wasn't about what I could get out of this lifelong covenant, but how I could serve Taylor. I had spent my first thirty-one years of life traveling all over the world, chasing a dream, growing a business, but it all paled in comparison to the decision I made on that summer evening.

It hit me: *my life now has purpose. My life has a purpose much bigger than myself.* Taylor isn't my Pippen or Shaq, she is my Jordan, my Kobe. I'm the background; without her by my side, there is no foreground.

To quote the last line of my vows, summing up everything I could possibly hope to learn in one lifetime about my own breakthrough purpose: "I've lived an amazing life, a life filled with adventure, a life filled with great accomplishments, but I never actually started living until today, the day I married you."

Why does the smile of the person you love make your purpose so clear?

BREAKTHROUGH PURPOSE KEYS

- Be the clutch player. Be relentlessly consistent.
- Live for the unseen hours.
- System + Process = Results.
- Focus on the fundamentals.
- Don't go through the motions. Commit.
- Create a legacy of leaders.
- Unconditional love is unconditional sacrifice.

BREAKTHROUGH PURPOSE TOOL: THE FIRST BITE

Why does that first bite always taste the best?

It's not your imagination. It really does flood your brain with dopamine; your body is rewarding you for nourishing it. The novelty heightens your senses, so you are tasting the fullness of the flavor, smelling every nuance of the aroma, and experiencing the rush of good feelings and memories tied to every delicious first bite you've had before.

And now that you've been handed the breakthrough formula that puts you on the path closer to reaching your dreams, you should get that same flood of excitement. You can't wait to dive in! Living a breakthrough day feels amazing!

But what happens with that second bite? And the third? And the thirty-third?

You're bored. Sensory-specific satiety: as you continue to consume the same thing, your senses adapt.

You can't ever let that thrill of your breakthrough purpose go stale. It requires rewiring your brain pretty frequently, but don't worry—it's easy and delicious. All it takes is a commitment to savoring the first bite of your last meal of the day.

Equipment Required: Dinner (preferably something healthy that you love)

Space Required: Anywhere

Time Required: <2 Minutes

Instructions:

1. Before you take your first bite of dinner (but after you are seated and have finished any blessings you make over your meals), take the time to really arrange the perfect first bite.

2. Pause and commit this bite to celebrating the ways that you have developed your breakthrough today.

3. Savor your first bite; this is the taste of your breakthrough purpose. Think about the ways you've developed your elite strengths, your breakthrough team, and the service you have done today.

4. As you finish the bite, take another short pause to accept today with gratitude, celebrate your breakthrough purpose with appreciation, and anticipate tomorrow with excitement.

CHAPTER 7

Conclusion: Full-Court Press

You've made it to the finish line! I've given you the tools to challenge your narratives, pivot your perspectives, think outside the proverbial box, and shift the paradigms you were previously taught. At your fingertips, you now have the power to integrate confidence, cooperation, service, and purpose into every aspect of your day, ultimately turning you into a breakthrough machine. Most people are too uncomfortable to question their status quo, to examine themselves and their lives for the gaps where breakthroughs are built. Not you. You explore the possibilities, you think differently, and that's worth celebrating!

But are you doing things differently yet?

Truthfully, there is no finish line to this program. I don't deal in short-term lifehacks. I don't write for armchair philosophers. The Breakthrough Blueprint is for BIOnic leaders—people who commit to their breakthroughs, people who think and take action. This is an amazing system, but you have to do the process yourself to get the results.

Will you have the breakthrough that solves your biggest challenge on your very first day? Maybe. Maybe not. Even if you do, are new breakthroughs going to be any less critical to your day tomorrow? Will your business stop needing innovation? Is your environment going to be any less disruptive and complex? Are you going to stop chasing exponential growth and improvement, professionally and personally? Was today the day that everything in your life stopped changing?

As long as you have a pulse, everything changes. Heck, I'm not even sure how many things I learned in kindergarten are still true. Is the brontosaurus still a dinosaur? Is Pluto still a planet? Have you heard that new, brain-breaking version of the Alphabet Song?!

Your senses have been your top resources for learning, living, and innovating from day one. Whatever disruptions the world has thrown at you, from solid foods to quarterly reports, you've been able to see, hear, sniff, taste, and touch your way through. They're the teachers who help you understand how dynamic and diverse your world is, the leaders who help you make every split-second decision, and your partners-in-crime as you make every memory.

Your brain pretty much never makes decisions based on the info you get from one sense alone. The senses are designed to work together. The Breakthrough Formula works the exact same way, igniting all your senses and infusing confidence, cooperation, service, and purpose into every area of your life.

But there's another sense. The sixth sense. No, not intuition, not ESP, not even seeing dead people, but *eminence*.

Eminence is a sense we are all born with, yet we never seem to fully grasp is actually within us. It is not greatness in the way we commonly think of the word. Eminence is becoming *obsessed* with the God-given gift you have been blessed with, that burning passion deep within your soul, and going all in. Searching, seeking, journeying across desolate lands far and wide to find what you were truly put on this earth to do! That is eminence.

You could be Bill Johnson, the best wool producer in the world who makes the softest cashmere deep in the mountains of Scotland. You could be Anne Jones, the lady who won the nation's best elementary school teacher 73 years in a row. You could be

Jiro from earlier in the book, the world's most precise, high quality fish selector creating artistry of life-changing sushi.

When did you stop dreaming? When the kid at school told you that you will never be an astronaut? When your parent yelled at you to 'get a real job?' When the outside world put so much pressure on you to fit the illuminated, circle-sized dream you had into a small, dark square cubicle?

You were given this gift for a reason and a purpose, there is no doubt about it. One of the greatest gratitude's we can give to God is by using the gift He has given us for the betterment of the people around us.

Not every moment will be a breakthrough. It just won't, and that's okay. But every day you implement the Breakthrough formula into your life, you will have moved one step closer to the breakthrough that is awaiting you. No one is a born loser. We lose confidence in ourselves, and on the impact we can have in the world. But no one has to live life feeling this way.

However, I must forewarn you there is actually a way to lose in life. Simply put, if you don't even give yourself a chance! If you give up and quit trying. If you succumb to the constant noise around you and try to be someone you're not and someone you don't even want to be. When you reject the gift you're given and your search for eminence, that's the only way you lose.

It doesn't matter where you came from or what your background is; you are called for greatness. It isn't easy, but we all have it inside of us. No matter how many people believe in you or how long it takes you to start, if you truly commit to this blueprint, you will break through. But only one person can make that choice for you: you. Breakthroughs rarely happen by accident—like, lottery odds (and how many lottery winners hit it big twice?!). Breakthroughs never happen just because you want them, but they can happen on demand. Not because you command them to appear out of thin air, but because you're strategically committed to a system and going through the process. You adopt the break-through formula because it is the answer to the biggest "how" of your life: how you become the breakthrough.

Most of the daily decisions you make don't instantly and drastically help or hurt your breakthrough. Committing to a daily routine with the Breakthrough Blueprint gives you the framework to make conscious decisions that constantly move the needle forward in the four most impactful breakthrough areas—and to make sure those decisions compound and develop on a schedule. You rise above your "how" to focus on what really matters, what actually optimizes the impact of your breakthroughs. In the process, you find the answers critical to breakthrough daily success and create the conditions in which breakthroughs not only can happen, but can come to life.

I'd love to tell you that the Breakthrough Blueprint will eventually become a habit. Everyone loves to talk about habits! But this routine never gets habitual and effortless. You need to consciously commit to it, every single day. It never gets any easier. But it not only delivers breakthrough results, it also makes everything in life more engaging, more exciting, more actionable, more fulfilling—and more rewarding.

Our brains die from the boredom of effortless routines, and our breakthroughs die right along with them. Don't make yourself a habit robot; don't mute your sensory input. Get comfortable getting uncomfortable. If you allow yourself to experience it, you can exponentially improve with every novel challenge. The leaps you take will no longer be daunting. You can embrace the challenge of living by the Breakthrough Blueprint, and breakthroughs themselves will become natural and easy, or you can continue throwing all your energy into the wind, hoping to attract a breakthrough. Don't underestimate even twenty-four hours of confidence, cooperation, service, and purpose.

As we wrap up this odyssey together, I want to leave you with this thought to digest until my next book comes out. Simply *knowing* is not enough.

The stoic philosophy that has become so popularized in the past years is flawed. Sorry Epicurus. Socrates, Aristotle, Plato, they missed the most important point of all. They based their teachings on *episteme* (the art of knowing). But what these great minds failed to realize, and what we still fail to realize today as a society, is that the real beauty and wisdom is found in the *techne* (the art of doing). Think about it, without doing there is nothing. Knowledge will always be there, taking action is for the chosen few. The chosen few who choose to DO!

And what greater form of gratitude could you give to your Creator than accepting the gift. He has given you and going *all in* to pursue it. Obsessed with finding the world's most rare nuts in South America? Do it! Obsessed with board games no one has ever heard of? Open a rare board game store.

Point being, we all have a God-given gift inside of us waiting to burst out. But yet far too many of us suppress it down, hide it like it doesn't exist. We never truly experience the feeling of *dying to live*. Instead we feel the constant day to day of *living to die*.

Put on your superhero cape of *choice*, tell the ancient philosophers to shove it, seek out the gift you have deep inside of you to make this world a better place, and get *doing*!

"For what it's worth ... it's never too late, or in my case too early, to be whoever you want to be. There's no time limit. Start whenever you want. You can change or stay the same. There are no rules to this thing. We can make the best or the worst of it. I hope you make the best of it. I hope you see things that startle you. I hope you feel things you never felt before. I hope you meet people who have a different point of view. I hope you live a life you're proud of, and if you're not, I hope you have the courage to start all over again."

—F. Scott Fitzgerald

ACKNOWLEDGMENTS

First and foremost I want to thank God, to whom I owe everything. Every day is an exciting journey on the mission you have gifted me! I am in awe of your greatness and the *amazing* blessings you continue to pour into my life.

To the love of my life, Taylor. I know I wouldn't have accomplished what I have without you. When I don't think I can do something, you believe in me. When I don't think I have energy in the tank, you encourage me. You are my rock; you are my everything!

To my puppy, Pivot. You are a ball of joy who absolutely lights up any situation. (And you were a rockstar salesman for *Pivot & Go!*) Thank you for joining our family and keeping me company while I write.

To my parents, Ann and Dan. You taught me at a young age to shoot for my dreams and never let anything or anyone make me feel like I couldn't accomplish them. I am forever grateful and thankful to you!

To my brother, Paul, and sister, Julia. Our sibling bond taught me what an amazing culture and breakthrough team should look like. Challenge *and* support!

To my editor, Lauren. Without you, the book wouldn't be the masterpiece it is!

To the Wiley team. It's a true gift from God to work with you guys and have you in my life. I'm forever grateful to you for this book and many more to come!

Special thanks to *all* the NBA players mentioned in this book who have trusted me to help shape their careers. To all the leaders and driven friends mentioned in this book who have pushed me to strive for new heights. To everyone mentioned in this book for the positive impact you have had on my life. To all of the teams and companies who have brought me in to speak and entrusted me with their culture. Thank you and thank you some more.

To the people who have given me opportunities to share this message, especially Edwin Arroyave, Jon Gordon, Lewis Howes, Jim Kwik, Brad Lomenick, David Meltzer, Jordan Montgomery, Ed Mylett, Carey Nieuwhof, Jim Rome, Jayson Waller, Steve Weatherford, and Eric Wood.

To all of my family around the world who have given me couches to sleep on, warm meals to eat, and loving, serving hands to help me along my journey, and to the people who believed in me through the years, including Ron Adams, Steve Alford, the Brooklyn Nets, Cori Close, Mark Dyer, John Farwell, Roger Fields, Kathryn Gordon, Archie McEachern, Gary Sacks, Ed Schilling, Erik Spoelstra, Jonathan Trent, Autumn Udell, Casey Wasserman, and Kris Weems.

To everyone who has ever believed in me. Thank you. I am forever grateful!

INDEX